# QUILTING FROM THE HEARTLAND

## by Sharlene Jorgenson

I would like to thank the following
people for all their invaluable  help and encouragement.

First of all my husband Mike, who has been most helpful and supportive. My children, for all of their encouragement and understanding. Phyllis Petersen, Esther Grischowsky, Dalene Thomas, and Julie Borge for all of the sewing they did to help prepare for the series. Margaret Lykins and Judith Dove for editing the book.

## PRODUCTION CREW  FOR TV SERIES
**Producers:** David E. and Kathryn Larson
**Editor:** Peter Pfankuck
**Director:** Ivy Lynn Revolinski
**Engineer/Technical Director:** John Kraft
**Floor Director:** Jim Lillis
**Lighting:** Andy Stieber
**Camera Operators:** Andy Stieber, Tom Reardon,
Jeff Cartier,
Pat Pfankuck, David C. Larson
**Photographer for "Quilting From the Heartland" book:** Jim Lillis & Jeff Silker

# QUILTING FROM THE HEARTLAND

# PREPARATION OF TEMPLATES USED IN ALL 13
## QUILT PROJECTS OF THIS BOOK

The templates come with a protective paper on each side; simply peel it off before using them. The templates are pink in color so that you don't lose them while working with them, as well as transparent so that you can take advantage of a certain design in the fabric.

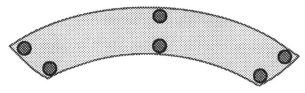

To give you the ultimate of accuracy while cutting with the Rotary Cutter, apply fabric grips to **each of the corners and if it's a larger piece put one in the middle of the edges of all of the templates.** This will keep them from sliding on your fabric while cutting. Caution! If you don't put the grips on the far corners the fabric will move when you get to them with the cutter. Fabric Grips are small circles of sandpaper with an adhesive backing.

To make it easier to identify the templates, label them with the letters shown on the templates in the diagrams at the beginning of each of the chapters in the supply lists. You can use a permanent marking pen or masking tape and a pen to do this.

## PREPARATION OF FABRICS USED IN ALL QUILTS

100% cotton fabric is the best to use in making a quilt. If you are going to use blends use fabrics of all the same blend. Separate the fabric by color (all the reds together etc.) and wash them in cool water with a mild soap that has no bleaching additives in it. If the fabric still bleeds you may have to wash it more than once. Line dry the fabric or put in an automatic dryer.

Iron the fabric so that there won't be any wrinkles to smooth out when getting ready to cut. Oops! If you like to use a steam iron when you are piecing a quilt and haven't pre-washed the fabric, you will have a whole new set of problems. I can tell you from experience that the fabrics will shrink when ironed with steam and they will also shrink more in one direction than another. This makes the pieces very difficult to work with.

## GENERAL DIRECTIONS FOR STRAIGHTENING THE FABRIC

Fold the fabric in half matching up the selvage edges. Position the folded fabric on the Matt Board so it extends to the right for right-handed people and to the left for left-handed

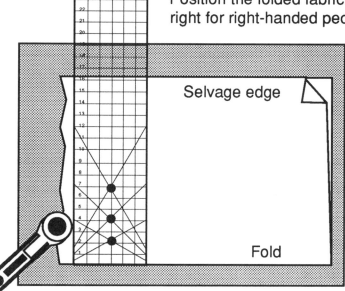

people. Place the bottom edge of the 6" x 24" Omnigrid ruler along the fold of the fabric in far enough from the uneven edge so that you can cut it off. Make a clean cut through the fabric, starting in front of the fold cutting to the opposite edge with one clean (not short and choppy) stroke. Always cut away from yourself. Try not to disturb the fabric after you have straightened this edge. It helps if you can bifold (fold on top of itself) your fabric on top of the board so you can easily turn the board without moving the fabric.

Selvage edge

Fold

# GENERAL DIRECTIONS FOR CUTTING STRIPS

Move the ruler to the proper position to get the width needed for the strips. Continue cutting until you have the required number of strips.

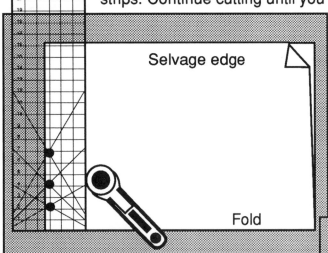

When you get more experienced with this method of straightening the fabric and cutting strips, you can layer several layers of folded fabrics on top of each other (as many as four fabrics if you are using the large Rotary Cutter) and cut many strips at a time. You might want to start out with two fabrics and work up to more.

If you are using a 6" x 12" Omnigrid ruler you will have to fold the fabric in half matching the selvage edge and in half again. Caution! You need to be careful that your fabric is lying straight so that you don't end up with zig zag strips when you cut them this way.

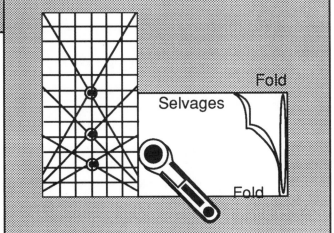

# CUTTING & SEWING TIPS

Always allow plenty of room in your work space to turn the Matt Board Cutting Base so you don't have to disturb the fabric, rulers, or templates. Matt Boards come in several sizes; use the one that fits the template you are working with.

When cutting around templates, I always make my first cut going backwards off of the fabric. Then, starting in the same place, I continue to cut away from myself.

Make sure you have the Fabric Grips on the templates. You might find the grips helpful also on your rulers.

Sew all seams with a scant 1/4" seam allowance to make up for the amount of fabric used in the seam line.

Finger press the seams before ironing by scratching the fabric of the seam line pushing it in the direction that you want it to go. This will give you more accuracy and speed when ironing and it will also eliminate those pleats we don't want after the strips are ironed.

I finger pin (holding the seams in place with my fingers when approaching them with the presser foot) when I feel that it isn't necessary to use pins. Pins aren't always needed.

Don't use nails; instead use #5003 IBC silk pins when you need to use pins, giving you more accuracy and the ability to sew over them if you wish.

To save time and thread, chain sew (means to continue to sew pieces together without stopping to cut the threads between each set of pieces).

# THE DOUBLE WEDDING RING

## Supplies Needed:
* Quick Strip™ templates QS1
* Small Rotary Cutter
* Fabric Grips (2 Pkg.)
* IBC Glass Head Pins #5003
* General Sewing Supplies
* Large Matt Board Cutting Base
* Omnigrid Ruler 6" x 24" or 6" x 12"
* Small Matt Board Base (9" x 12")

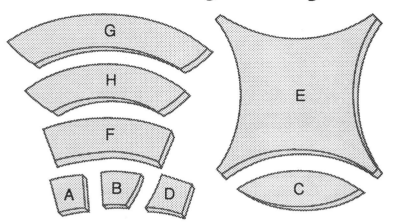

**READ PAGES 3 - 14 BEFORE STARTING THE QUILT.**
**CHOOSING FABRICS**
**FOR THE SCRAP VARIATION OF THE DOUBLE WEDDING RING**

Step #1

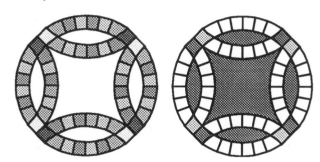

Step #1. Remember, scraps can be beautiful, and this quilt will give you a chance to use scraps left over from other sewing projects. I have made the Double Wedding Ring using only stripes and plaids or mixed them in with other fabrics and it looks great.

You need to decide if you want to put the light fabrics on a dark background or dark fabrics on a light background. For the connecting corners you want to choose fabrics of a high contrast so that the circles are more defined.

Step #2. You might want to separate the light scrap fabrics ￼brics so that you don't get the missing tooth effect.

Step #2

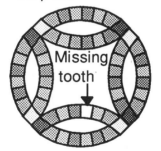

TING INSTRUCTIONS FOR A SCRAP DOUBLE WEDDING RING
**FINISHED SIZE 47 1/4" X 47 1/4"**

Step #3. Template G is the most efficient template to use from the QS1 pattern when cutting up scraps. Place 6 layers of fabric on top of each other. Don't be concerned about the order they are in or whether there is enough fabric to fill the whole arc you are going to cut. You will discard the unfilled pieces when you begin to sew the Double Wedding Ring together.

Place template G on top of the 6 layers of fabric and cut around it with the small Rotary Cutter. I don't pay attention to the grain line when cutting these pieces.

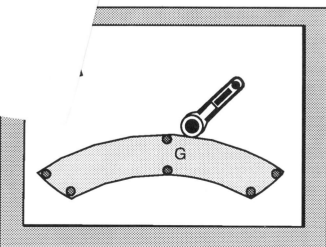

Leave plenty of room on your work surface to turn the cutting board as you work your way around the template. I find it works best if I bifold the fabric up so all of it is on top of the board. This makes it easier to turn the board as I work. <u>Do not disturb this arc until you have completed the next step.</u>

Step #4

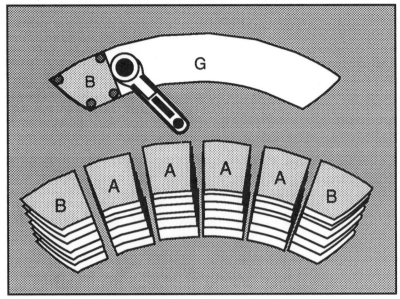

Step #4. Next cut the end off of the arc with template B and the four center wedges with template A. Template B should also fit the opposite end of the arc. If it doesn't you have let something slip and you need to check which ones have been cut wrong. <u>You will get 36 pieces from one cutting if all of the pieces filled out, or enough for 6 arcs of the scrap Double Wedding Ring.</u> Repeat these steps 14 times.

To help you evenly distribute the scrap pieces through out the whole quilt, divide the piles of the four center wedges into four containers and work with pieces from one container at a time when sewing the pieces together. Put the right and left B pieces into separate containers.

## CUTTING THE CONNECTING CORNERS

Step #5. It's hard to pick the connecting corner colors so you might want to sew a few arcs together before you cut them out. Refer to the top of page 9 before you continue. Going from selvage to selvage cut 4 strips 3" wide of each of the fabrics used for the connecting corners. Refer to pages 3-4 to see how to straighten the fabric and how to cut the strips you need. Place 2 strips of each of the colors used on top of each other and bifold the fabric so that it fits on top of the mat board that you are going to use. I prefer to use a smaller board (9" x 12") for this part making it easier to turn as I cut around the template D.

Step #5

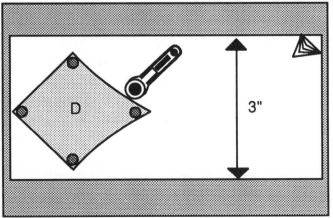

There are two ways in which you can cut the connecting corners, on the straight of grain or on the bias. Place the D as shown in the diagram to the left to cut it on the bias. I prefer the bias because the pieces are easier to sew into the quilt making the small amount of fabric wasted worthwhile. To cut on the straight of grain line up one of the straight edges of the template D with the bottom of the strips. These strips would only have to be cut 2 1/2" wide.

Cut 46 D's of each color.

6

## CUTTING THE BACKGROUND AND MELONS

Step #6

Fold

Fold

C
C E C
C
C
C E C
C

Step #6. Fold the fabric in half matching up the selvage edges. Then fold the fabric a second time so that you have four thicknesses. Make sure that the fabric is lying nice and flat before you begin to cut.

Use template E to cut the backgrounds and template C to cut the melons. You will waste very little fabric when you cut these pieces together taking advantage of the curves. Cut the 16 E's out first on the big matt board. Allow yourself plenty of room to turn the board as you work.

Pay attention to the grain line of the fabric when you cut out these two pieces.

After you are done cutting out the E pieces, move the left over pieces of fabric to a smaller matt board and cut out 40 melons. I like to work on the smaller board because it is easier to turn.

Sometimes the fabric will not be wide enough to cut C's on both sides of the E template. When this happens you will have to cut one set along the edge and a single one out of the folded edge when laid out flat.

## GIVE YOURSELF A SEWING TEST
## BEFORE STARTING CONSTRUCTION

Even though the 1/4" seam allowance is included in the templates, you can't sew with the full 1/4" seam. You must make up for the amount of fabric used up in the seam line when making the seams. Therefore, we tell you to sew with a **scant 1/4"** seam allowance so that everything is perfectly fit.

Step #7. Before you go too far I want you to give yourself a sewing test. Sew one arc together first like the diagram on the right. Iron the seams as indicated in the drawing and place the sewn arc on top of template H (also called the seamless arc template), to see if all six pieces sewn together fit the template. If they don't, adjust your seam allowance so that these pieces fit. If your seam allowance is incorrect throughout the quilt you will have puckering in the seam lines.

Step #7

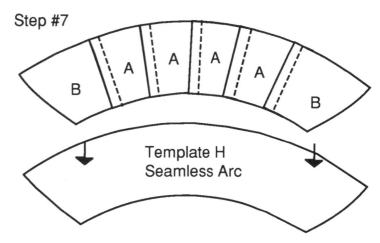

Now that you have passed your sewing test you can continue on without any concerns about the pieces fitting together.

## CHAIN SEWING THE A'S TOGETHER

Step #8

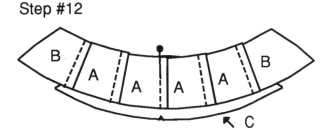

Step #8. Even though this a scrap quilt, I try to place the pieces in the arcs so that there is a contrast of color and print throughout the design.

Picking the pieces up in no particular order start to chain sew the A's together.

Step #9. Chain sew until there are 4 A's in the center of each arc. **Do not back stitch** as it will only create bulk in the corners. Make 80 arcs with 4 A's in them.

Step #9

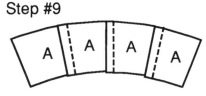

## ADD THE B PIECE TO EACH END OF THE ARC

Step #10

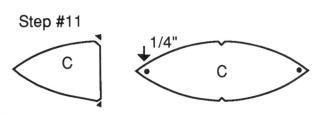

Step #10. With right sides together place the only straight edge of a B piece on top of the straight edge of one of the A pieces at the end of the arc and sew this seam. Repeat this step on the other end of the arc. If you passed the sewing test you can chain sew working with all 80 arcs, saving time and thread. Iron these seams to the left as shown in the diagram above.

## ADD THE MELON TO ONE SIDE OF THE ARC

Step #11. Find the center of the melon or piece C by folding it in half. Cut a very small notch on the folded edge to mark the middle on both sides of the melon. Be very careful not to cut this notch too big going into the seam line. This, too, is only done to mark the center.

Step #11

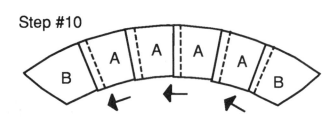

You could also mark this point with a fabric marking pencil or pin. Make a dot 1/4" in on the points of the C piece with a fabric marking pencil.

Step #12. To half (40) of the arcs add a melon. With the right sides together place the pieced arc on the top of the melon, matching the center seam of the arc to the notch of the melon. Place the first pin in the middle to hold it in place. Next place a pin on each end. The melon will overlap the edge by 1/4" when pinned, because the seam allowance is included. Put one more pin in between the end and middle on both sides. Sew this seam with the pieced arc on top for best results. Because you ironed the seams of the arc to the left earlier you don't have to sew against them now.

Step #12

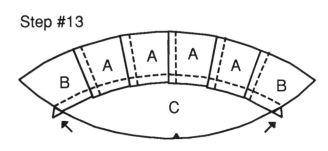

Step #13. Iron the seam allowance of this step towards the C or melon. Notice that the tips of the melon are extended after this step is ironed.

Step #13

8

# ADDING THE CONNECTING CORNERS

Sometimes when I get to this step in sewing the Double Wedding Ring I change my mind about the color I'm going to use for the connecting corners. I experiment with some different color combinations before I cut them all.

#14
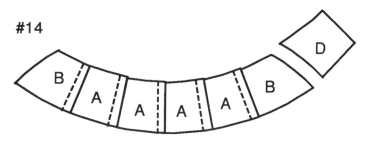

Step #14. To the other half (40) of the pieced arcs, attach the connecting corners (the D piece) with different colors on opposite ends. Be careful to match up the right curve of the B piece to the right curve of the D piece as shown in Step # 14.

#15
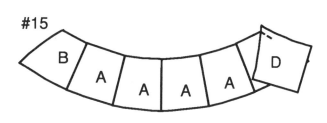

Step #15. With right sides together place the D on top of the B. The connecting corner D piece will extend over the top edge 1/4" when it is lined up right. **Do not back stitch.** Without using pins, sew just a few stitches and stop with the needle in the down position. Lift the pressure foot.

#16
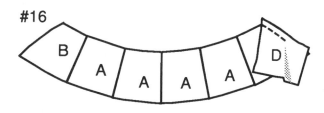

Step #16. Readjust the edges of the D to fit the curve of the B piece on the underside and sew a few more stitches as shown. Leave the needle down and lift the pressure foot. Adjust the edges of the D to line up with the B the rest of the way.

#17
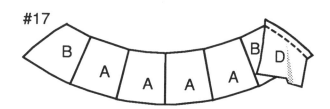

Step #17. Drop the pressure foot and finish this seam. **Do not back stitch.** When you get used to this technique you will agree that pins would be in the way for this seam.

Repeat this step on the opposite end of the arc.

#18
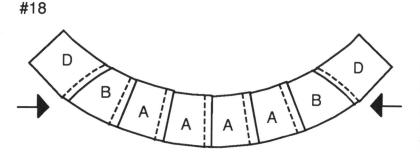

Step #18. Iron the seams of the D's towards the center as shown in the diagram to the left. Do not stretch the arc when pressing the seams.

**9**

# CONNECTING THE TWO PARTS OF THE MELON

**Step #19**

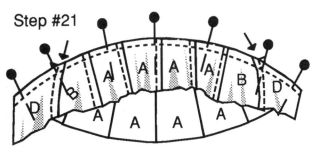

**Step #20**

match center seam on top
to the notch on piece C
on the bottom

**Step #21**

**Step #22**

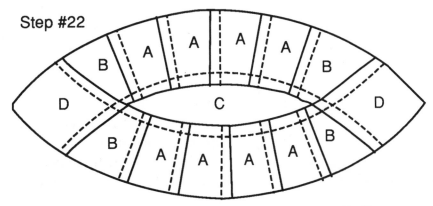

Step #19. You are now ready to sew the two sections together in one continuous seam.

I recommend that you use the IBC # 5003 Glass Head silk pins for all pinning in this design. If the shaft of the pin is too large you will lose some of the accuracy when you sew over the pins.

Step #20. With right sides together place the pieced arc with the connecting corners on the top. Match the center seam of the pieced arc up to the notch of the C piece on the bottom and pin in place.

Step #21. Look at the arrows in Step #19. Stick a pin on the seam line 1/4" in from the edge between piece D and B bringing it through to 1/4" in from the edge on the seam line between C and B on the bottom. Next turn the tip of the pin up through the fabric. You do not need to be concerned where it comes through. Repeat this step on the other end of the arc. Also pin the very ends of the D's and B's together and a couple more in between as shown in Step #21.
**Do not back stitch** at the beginning and end of this seam. Sew this seam sewing **directly over the point the pin goes in.** This is indicated by the arrows in diagram #3. This makes the perfect corners.

Step #22. Press this seam towards the C. If the melon does not lay flat your seam allowance has been too big or too small.

**10**

# ATTACHING THE BACKGROUNDS

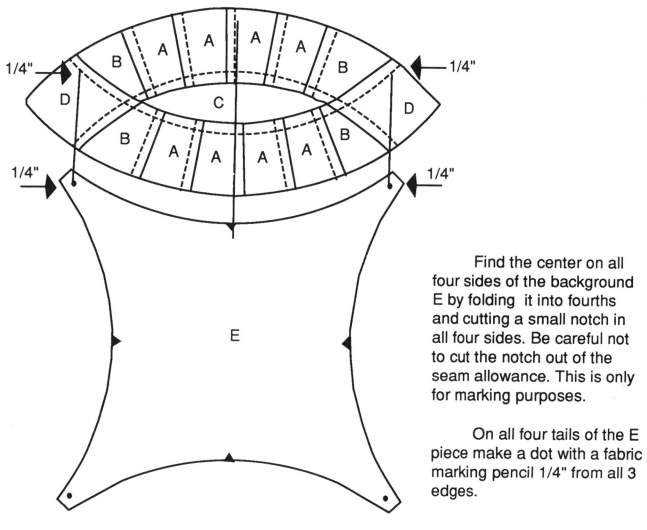

Find the center on all four sides of the background E by folding it into fourths and cutting a small notch in all four sides. Be careful not to cut the notch out of the seam allowance. This is only for marking purposes.

On all four tails of the E piece make a dot with a fabric marking pencil 1/4" from all 3 edges.

With the right sides together and the **background E on top,** match up the center seam line of the pieced melon to the notch on the E background piece. Pin both corners of the background at the dots to the melon on the seam line 1/4" from the edge between D and B.

Back stitch to the point where the pin goes in. Sew to the other corner and back stitch. It is very important that you **sew only to the point where the pin goes in** for perfect corners. You **never** sew to the end of the E piece.

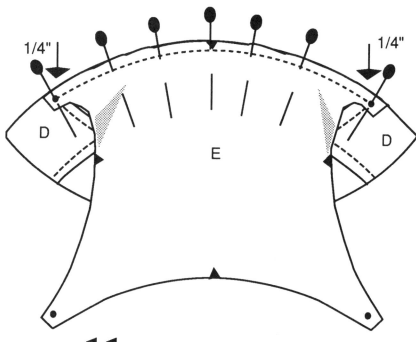

**11**

## ATTACHING THE SECOND MELON

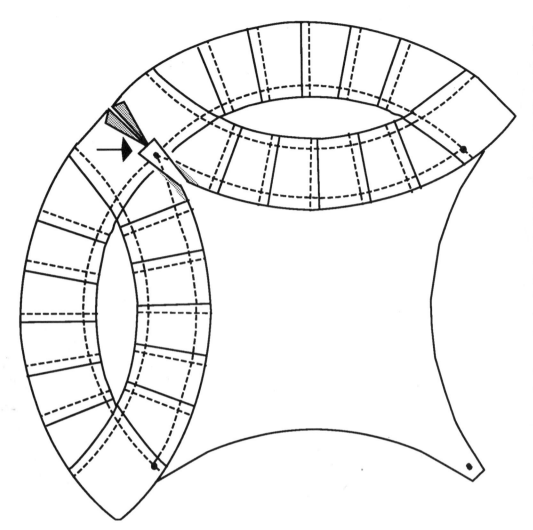

When you add the second, third, and fourth melon it works best to add them going counter-clockwise. Always sew with the E background on top and **never** sew to the end of the background tails where indicated by the arrow. Press these seams towards the center background E. In the corners fold the seam back where the arrow is pointing. Do not sew the D's together yet. This isn't done until the rows are connected.

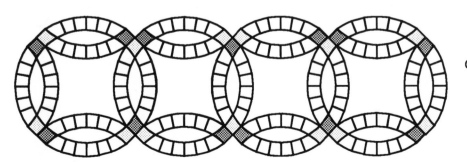

After you have made one complete circle, make the connecting circle with three sides. You want to make sure that you lay out the melons ahead of time so that the colors of the connecting corners alternate correctly. If you should happen to make one wrong, don't rip it apart because it will fit the next space. When you add the connecting circle, sew with the E background on top and stop at each dot. Do not sew the connecting corners yet.

Make this row 4 circles long.

**12**

# CONNECTING THE ROWS

With right sides together place the E's on top of row 2 and match up the center seams of the melon's to the notches on the E pieces. Put a pin in each center and at each corner connecting the dots on the E to the seam line between D and B. Treat each circle as a separate seam and back stitch at each dot. Do not sew through the tails of the E piece and do not sew the connecting corners until the row is completed.

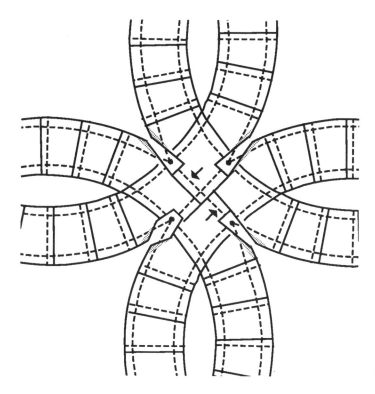

## SEWING AND PRESSING THE CONNECTING CORNERS

The very last seams are the connecting corners at the intersections of the circles. I suggest you do the corners as you connect the rows so you don't have to handle so much bulk.

First sew the two sets of seams across from each other indicated by the arrows. When you sew these seams, start from the center and sew towards the dot and back stitch. Notice how the tail of the E is not included in this seam. Bend it back out of the way when you approach the corner.

Next, sew the last seam across the middle, flip flopping the seams of the intersection in opposite directions. Back stitch at each end of this seam.

Press the tails of the E open and flat like the drawing to the left shows. Notice how the seams meet at the dot in each corner.

13

## ADDING THE D'S ON THE OUTSIDE EDGE

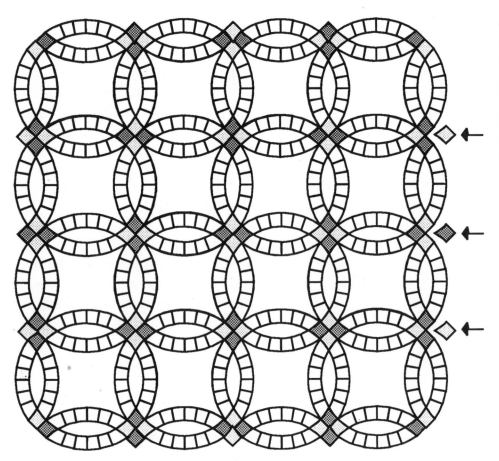

Adding the extra connecting corners on the outside edge of the quilt is optional. These are added after the quilt has reached it's finished size.

**FINISHED SIZE OF THIS WALL QUILT 47 1/4" X 47 1/4"**
**IT IS PICTURED IN THE COLOR SECTION OF THIS BOOK**

## YARDAGE REQUIREMENTS:

1 1/4 yd. Background E fabric and C
1/3 yd. of two colors for connecting corners
1/2 yd. each of 6 fabrics if your using new fabrics for the arcs or
1/4 yd. of 12 fabrics for the arcs
1 3/4 yd. for the backing and binding

I used 30 different *fat quarters of new fabric for the arcs, blue for the back ground, and yellow and red connecting corners, all resembling prints and colors of the 30's.

*fat quarters are 18" x 22 1/2" cut pieces of fabric sometimes available at your local quilt shop.

# THE GLORIFIED NINE PATCH

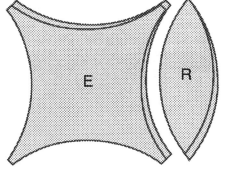

## Supplies Needed:

*E Background template from QS1
*Add On template R from QS2
*IBC Glass Head Pins #5003
*Large Matt Board Cutting Base
*Small Matt Board Base 9" x 12"
*Omnigrid Ruler 6" x 24" or 6" x 12"
*Omnigrid Ruler 12 1/2" x 12 1/2"
*Omnigrid Ruler 1" x 12"

**READ PAGES 3 - 4 BEFORE STARTING THE QUILT.**

### CHOOSING FABRICS FOR THE GLORIFIED NINE PATCH

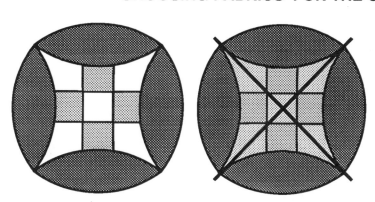

In each nine patch you want to use fabrics with a variety of background and print so that the pieces in the nine patch can be identified. The more contrast you use in color, the better the quilt will look. I do prefer using scraps for this quilt or enough variety of new fabrics so that it appears to look old. It is always much easier to choose the fabrics for the melons after all of the nine patches are made.

### CUTTING STRIPS FOR THE NINE PATCHES
### THE FINISHED SIZE OF THIS QUILT WILL BE 46" X 46"

Because I prefer to use so many different fabrics for this design, I worked with 26 different *fat quarters for this quilt. There will be one nine patch left over for a pillow, because you will only use 25 of the 26 uneven nine patches.

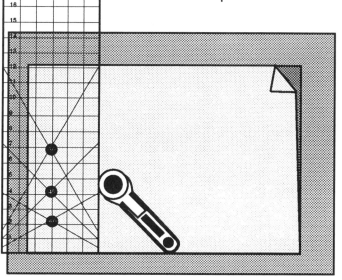

Pair up the fabrics into 13 sets making sure that there is a high contrast in print and color between the two fabrics. Set all the paired sets of fabric aside after they are pinned together and work with just one set at a time.

To save time, lay both of the fat quarter fabrics from one set on top of each other so you can cut the strips for combination 1 and 2 at the same time.

Before you begin to cut the strips, straighten one edge of the fat quarters. Never use the selvage edge of the fabric in a quilt.

Step 1

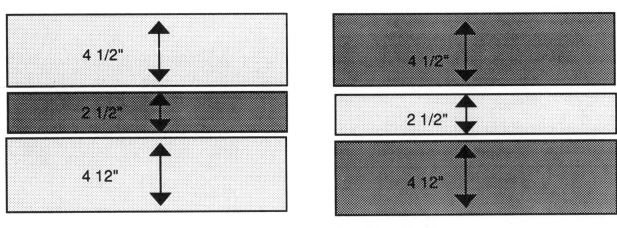

Combination 1                                    Combination 2

Step 1. Cut two sets of 4 1/2" strips and one set of 2 1/2" strips from each one of the sets of paired up fat quarters. When steps 1-5 are completed you will get 2 uneven nine patches from combination 1 and 2. These will be opposite each other giving you more variety of blocks in your quilt.

Step 2

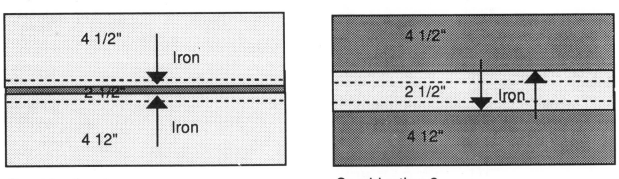

Combination 1                                    Combination 2

Step 2. With a scant 1/4" seam allowance sew both a combination 1 and combination 2 from the set of strips you cut in step 1. It is not necessary to pin before sewing these seams. Finger press the seams first to set the seams in the direction that you want them to go. Then Iron them. The seams of Combination 1 go towards the center and the seams of Combination 2 towards the outside edge. Repeat Step 1 and 2, thirteen more times, until you have used up all 26 fabrics.

Step 3

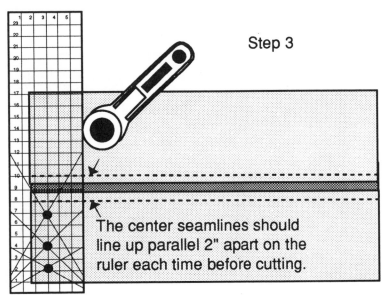

The center seamlines should line up parallel 2" apart on the ruler each time before cutting.

Step 3. Check each time before you cut a new strip that lines 2" apart on the ruler line up with the center seam lines on the combination you are cutting. Cut two 4 1/2" strips and one 2 1/2" strip from combination 1 and the same from combination 2.

# SEW THE UNEVEN NINE PATCHES TOGETHER

## Step 4

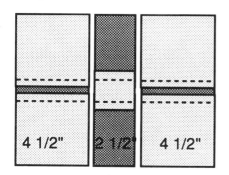

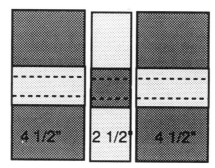

**Steps 4 & 5.** Using a scant 1/4" seam allowance sew the cut strips from step 3 together to form the uneven nine patches. If you have ironed the seams right the seams will lock together when you sew. It is not necessary to use pins for these seams. I just finger pin as I go.

You will get two uneven nine patches from each of the 13 paired sets of fabric you pinned together. The fabrics in the two blocks will be opposite of each other when sewn.

Now run the nail of your pointer finger along the seam line and finger press to set these seams towards the center. Press with the iron.

## Step 5

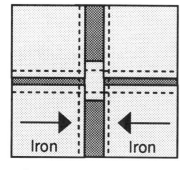

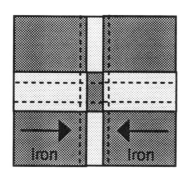

## SCORING TEMPLATE E

**Step 6.** Center template E on top of a 12 1/2" x 12 1/2" Omnigrid ruler. Score parallel lines 2" apart in the center of the template with a sharp object. Place a 1" x 12" ruler on top of the template to use when scoring these lines.

## Step 6

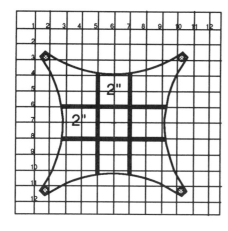

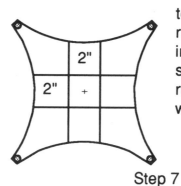

Step 7

## CUTTING THE UNEVEN NINE PATCH

**Step 7.** Center template E over the top of the nine patch and line up the scored lines on the template with the seam lines on the nine patch. You cannot cut more than one of these at a time because it would be impossible to line up the seams directly on top of each other. Do not disturb the fabric and template as you cut, but turn the board as you work your way around the template. It will be easier if you work on a smaller matt board.

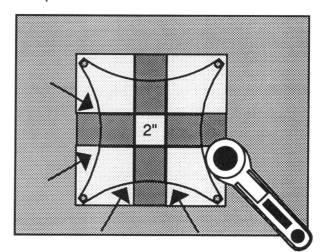

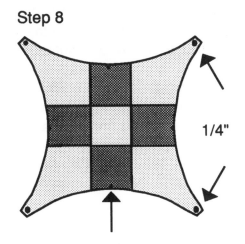

**Step 8**

1/4"

Step 8. With a fabric marking pencil mark a dot on all four corners of the background 1/4" in from all three sides of the tails. Mark the centers of all four sides of the uneven nine patch. It is easiest if you fold it in half and cut a **tiny** notch on each side and a second time folding the nine patch in the other direction to cut those notches.

## CUTTING THE R'S

Step 9. There are a couple of different ways to cut out the R's. I recommend you read this complete section on cutting them before continuing.

To avoid working with large amounts of fabric when cutting out the R's, I first cut the fabric into strips going from selvage to selvage. Refer to pages 3 & 4 to see how to cut the strips.

**Step 9**

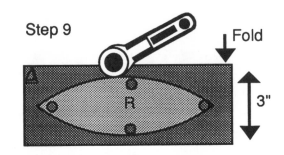

Fold

3"

If you cut the strips 3 1/2" wide you need to cut 15 strips for this quilt. Fold each strip in half and in half a second time so you cut 4 R's at one time. Place the template R in a horizontal position. This method wastes a little more fabric than the next one.

If you cut the strips 10" wide you need to cut 5 strips. Layer all 5 strips on top of each other so you will save time. Place template R in a vertical position and begin to cut with the Rotary Cutter. I prefer this method.

**Step 9**

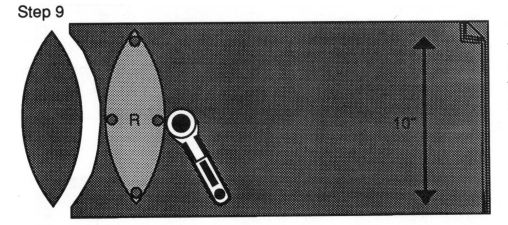

10"

Work on a 9" x 12' Matt Board base when cutting the R's so you can easily turn the board when cutting.

Cut 60 R's.

**Step 10**

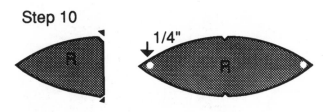

1/4"

Step 10. Find the center of the R's by folding it in half. Cut a very small notch on the folded edge to mark the middle on both sides of the melon. Be careful not to cut the notch too big. Next use a fabric marking pencil to put a dot on each point of the melon 1/4" in from the two edges. Test the pencil first on a scrap of fabric to make sure that the mark can be removed.

**18**

Step 11

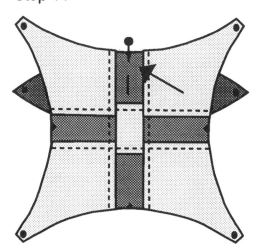

## SEWING THE MELONS TO THE BACKGROUND

Step 11. With the right sides together and the uneven nine patch on the top, match up the notch on the nine patch to the notch on the melon. Put a pin in the center. If you use the recommended silk pins your corners will come together into nicer points. Some pins available are almost like nails and you can't sew over them or up to them.

Step 12

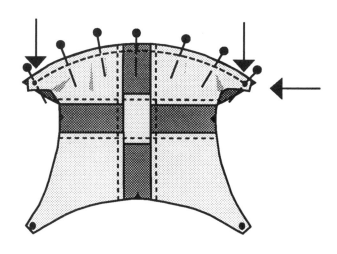

Step 12. Match up the dot on the background to the dot on the melon and pin. Do this to both ends. Put a couple more pins in between the ends and the middle on both sides. Notice that there will be a little of the tip of the melon showing when pinned. Back stitch to the dot and sew to the other end and again back stitch.

## MAKING THE ROWS

Even though we are working with a quilt that has a traditional scrap look to it, we want to make sure that we like certain blocks next to each other. Lay all of the nine patches on top of a bed sheet in the desired order and pin.

Add the second, third, and fourth melon to the nine patches always working with the background on the top. Always back stitch to each corner through the construction of the rest of this quilt.

Add the second row and continue to add rows until you have the fifth row added.

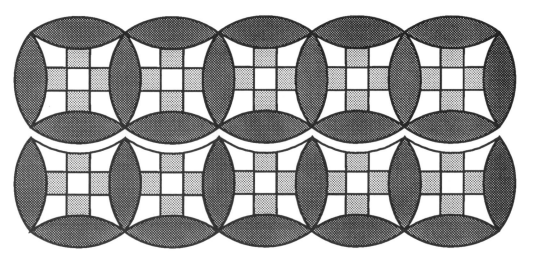

**19**

# GLORIFIED NINE PATCH

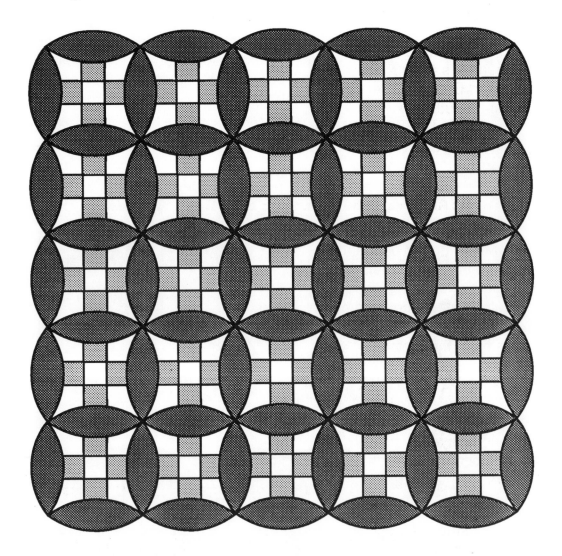

**FINISHED SIZE OF THIS QUILT IS 46" X 46"**
**IT IS PICTURED IN THE COLORED SECTION OF THIS BOOK**

## YARDAGE REQUIREMENTS:

26 different fat quarters
1 3/4 yd. for the melons
3 yds. for the back
1 1/2 for the binding

*Fat quarters are 18" x 22 1/2" cut pieces of fabric sometimes available at your local quilt shop.

You can also make this quilt using the same fabrics in every nine patch.

# DIAMOND DOUBLE WEDDING RING

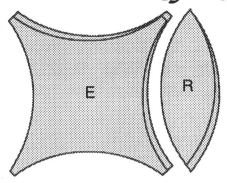

## Supplies Needed:

*E template from QS1
*Add On template R from QS2
*IBC Glass Head Pins #5003
*Large Matt Board Cutting Base
*Small Matt Board Cutting Base 9" x 12"
*Omnigrid Ruler 6" x 24" or 6" x 12"
*Omnigrid Ruler 1" x 12"
*Rotary Cutter

**READ PAGES 3 - 4 BEFORE STARTING THE QUILT.**

## SELECTING THE FABRICS
### FOR THE DIAMOND DOUBLE WEDDING RING

You will need four different fabrics for the melons of this pattern. You'll want to experiment with different fabric placements to create a melon that is exciting and pleasing to you. Use fabrics with high contrast from light to dark and with a variety of prints and backgrounds. I have found this design to be most pleasing when I put the brightest colors on the ends of melons and use the same fabric for the centers of the melons and the background.

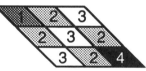

## PLAN AHEAD AND SAVE TIME WHEN CUTTING THE STRIPS

Fold each of your four different fabrics in half with the selvage edges together. You will need the most strips of fabric #2 so put it on the bottom. Next put fabric #3 and follow with the fabric #1 & #4 from which you need the same number of strips.

After the fabrics are straight and in the right order, bifold them so that they all fit on top of the large Matt Board Cutting Base. This makes it easier to turn the board. You do not want to disturb the fabric after you have straightened the edge. Refer to page 4 and 5 for instructions on cutting strips.

With the large Rotary Cutter cut 2" strips through all the layers of fabric. After you have cut 6 strips remove fabrics #1 & #4. Continue cutting 2" strips until you have a total of 18 strips of # 3 fabric. Remove #3 and cut 2" strips until you have 24 strips of #2 fabric.

## NUMBER OF E'S AND STRIPS TO CUT FOR THE FOUR COLOR NINE PATCHES
### FINISHED QUILT SIZE 55" X 55"

**NUMBER OF STRIPS & E'S TO CUT**

◼ Fabric 1 Cut 6-2" strips
▨ Fabric 2 Cut 24-2" strips
☐ Fabric 3 Cut 18-2" strips
◼ Fabric 4 Cut 6-2" strips
☐ Fabric 3 Cut 36 E's (read step #1 page 22 before cutting these

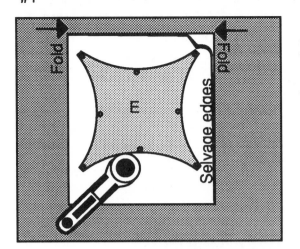

## CUTTING THE BACKGROUND E'S

Step #1. Fold the #3 fabric in half, and in half again. Place template E on top and cut around it with the small Rotary Cutter. Make sure you have plenty of room to turn the board as you cut around the template. You will get 4 each time. Cut 36 E's.

## SEW THE COMBINATION STRIPS TOGETHER

Step #2. Following the fabric #'s on the diagrams below, sew these sets of fabric strips together until you have 6 of each of the combinations. To save material off set each of the strips 1 3/4" as shown. Finger press, then iron as indicated by the arrow in each combination.

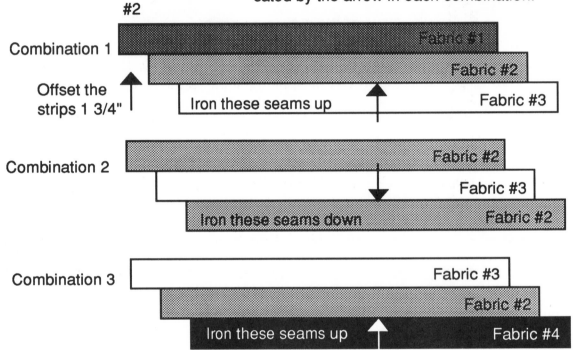

Combination 1

Offset the strips 1 3/4"

Fabric #1
Fabric #2
Iron these seams up
Fabric #3

Combination 2

Fabric #2
Fabric #3
Iron these seams down
Fabric #2

Combination 3

Fabric #3
Fabric #2
Iron these seams up
Fabric #4

## CUT THE COMBINATION STRIPS AT THE 45° ANGLE

Step #3. Place the 45° angle of the ruler on a middle seam line of one of the combination strips and trim off the uneven end. Move the ruler over 2" and cut your first strip. You will get 14 of the 2" strips from each combination. When cutting these strips, keep checking to see if the 2"

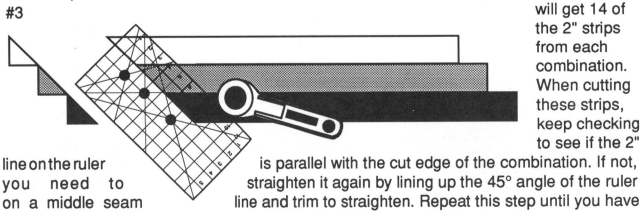

line on the ruler you need to on a middle seam cut up all of the combi-

is parallel with the cut edge of the combination. If not, straighten it again by lining up the 45° angle of the ruler line and trim to straighten. Repeat this step until you have nation strips.

22

#4

Combinations 1 2 3

## SEW THE NINE PATCHES TOGETHER

Step #4. Take a strip from combinations 1, 2, & 3 and lay them in piles in front of you in the correct order so you will be less apt to sew them together incorrectly. There should be 84 in each pile.

Step #5. With right sides together place combination 2 on top of combination 1 and insert the pins on the seam lines 1/4" from the cut edge on the top and bottom strip. It is only important where the pin **goes in** the fabric not where it comes out.

#5     #6

Step #6. Sew directly over the point where the pin goes in. Notice the beginning and end of each seam has a 1/4" tail extended.

Press these **seams open** to make step #9 easier.

Step #7. You will save a lot of time and thread if you chain sew the nine patches together. Sew 84 of these nine patches.

#7

#8

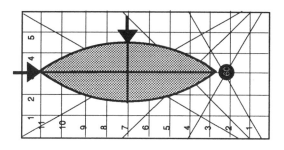

Step #8. Place template R on top of a 6" x 12" Omnigrid ruler and line up the points of template R with a horizontal line and the middle of the template with a vertical line on the ruler. Use a 1" x 12" ruler on top of the template as a guide to run a sharp object next to and score the template in both directions.

#9

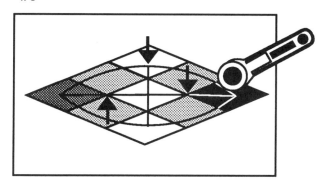

Step #9. Line up the scored lines on the template with the points on the nine patch indicated by the arrows in the diagram. If you work on a 9" x 12" Matt Board Base It will be much easier to turn as you cut around the template. Cut only one of these at a time.

**23**

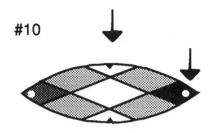

## MARKING THE R'S AND E'S

Step #10. Fold the melons in half and cut a small notch to mark the center. Also make a dot on both points of the melons 1/4" from the sides with a fabric marking pencil.

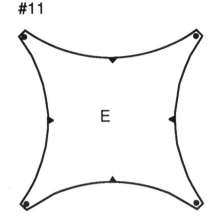

Step #11. Fold the E in fourths to find the center of the curved edges and cut a small notch. Put a dot in the middle of the tails of the Background E 1/4" from all three edges.

## SEWING THE MELONS TO THE BACKGROUNDS

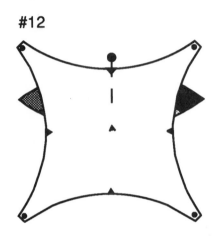

Step #12. With right sides together and the E on top match the notch of the E piece to the notch of the melon and pin.

Step #13. Match up the dot on the melon to the dot on the background E and pin. Put a couple more pins in between. You will be able to sew over the pins and the corners will also match better If you use silk pins. There will be a little tip of the melon showing when pinned. Back stitch to the dot and sew to the dot at the other end and back stitch.

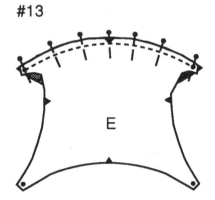

Step #14. When adding the nine patch melons you have to be sure that the #1 fabrics meet in the corners and the #4 fabrics meet in the corners. You will not get stars in the intersections If a melon is put in wrong.

Step #15. Always keeping the E piece on top, add the third and fourth melon. Keep adding melons and E pieces until this row is 6 circles long.

#15

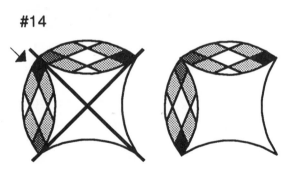

Step #16. Add the second row and continue to add rows until you have six rows.

# DIAMOND DOUBLE WEDDING RING

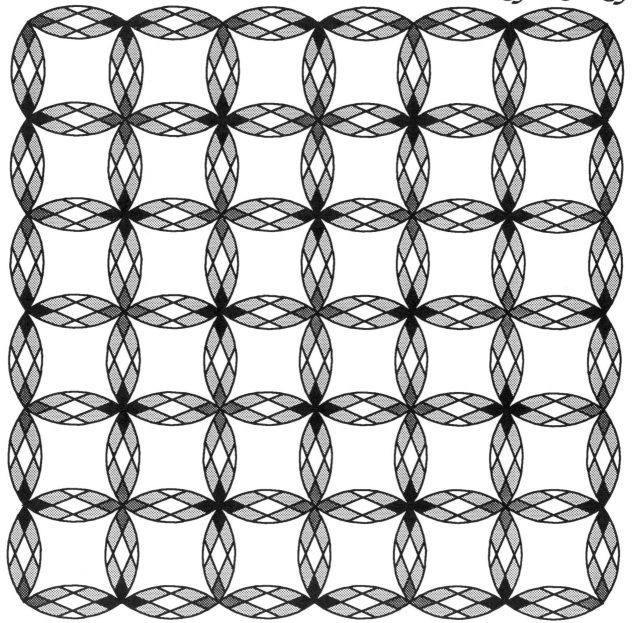

**FINISHED SIZE OF THIS QUILT IS 55" X 55"**
**IT IS PICTURED IN THE COLORED SECTION OF THIS BOOK**
## YARDAGE REQUIREMENTS:

1/2 yd. fabric 1
1 1/2 yds. fabric 2
1yd. fabric 3
1/2 yd. fabric 4
2 3/4 yd. fabric 3 for background
   3 1/2 yds. for back of quilt
   1 yd. for binding

   IF you were to change the background and the #3 fabric to dark and the #1 and #4 to bright fabrics and #2 to a medium color you will also have a beautiful color arrangement.

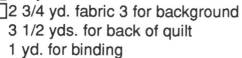

## 25

# STAR FLOWER.

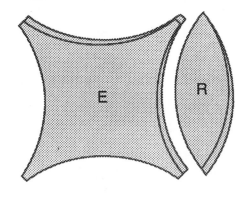

## Supplies Needed:
*E template from QS1
*Add On template R from QS2
*IBC Glass Head Pins #5003
*Large Matt Board Cutting Base
*Small Matt Board Cutting Base 9" x 12"
*6" x 12" Omnigrid Ruler with 45° angle marked
*Small Rotary Cutter is best
*General Sewing Supplies

## CHOOSING THE FABRICS

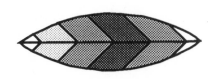

The more color you use in this quilt the better you will like it. Thinking of some of the bright colors you see in bird feathers or the rainbow might give you some ideas for picking colors for this quilt. Your design will be most effective if you put the brightest fabrics in the one and six position (look at the diagram below). IF fabric #1 is a bright rose color #2 could be a little darker and #3 still darker. If #6 were a bright teal green #5 could a medium teal and #4 still darker. Don't be afraid to make your own arrangement of colors. You should also use a variety of prints and backgrounds for more pleasing effects. Also when you examine the design you will see that one end of the melon looks like the point of an arrow and the other end looks like blades of a windmill.

### READ PAGES 3 AND 4 BEFORE STARTING THE QUILT.

### PLAN AHEAD AND SAVE TIME WHEN CUTTING THE STRIPS

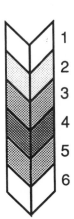

Before you begin to cut the strips you need to arrange the fabrics in the order that you want them in the melons and give them a number. To save time when cutting the strips for the melons (sometimes referred to as feathers) cut fabrics 1 & 6 at the same time because they are 2" wide and fabrics 2, 3, 4, & 5 at the same time as they will be cut 1 1/2" wide. Refer to pages 3 & 4 for instructions on cutting strips.

### NUMBER OF STRIPS & E'S TO CUT
### FINISHED SIZE OF THIS WALL QUILT WILL BE 46" X 46"

Fabric 1 cut 10 - 2" strips
Fabric 2 cut 10 -1 1/2" strips
Fabric 3 cut 10 -1 1/2" strips
Fabric 4 cut 10 -1 1/2" strips
Fabric 5 cut 10 -1 1/2" stirps
Fabric 6 cut 10 - 2" strips
Background fabric cut 25 E's (read step #1 page 27 before cutting these)

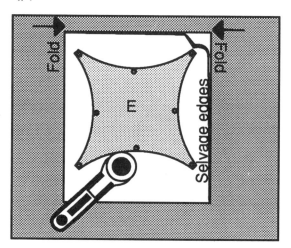

#1

## CUTTING THE BACKGROUND E'S

Step # 1. Fold the fabric in half, and in half again. Place template E on top and cut around it with the small Rotary Cutter. Make sure you have plenty of room to turn the board as you cut around the template. You will get 4 each time. Cut 25 E's.

## SEW THE COMBINATION STRIPS TOGETHER

Step #2. Using a scant 1/4" seam allowance, sew the strips together following the order shown in the diagrams below. Off set each of the strips 1" when sewing them together to save fabric when cutting them at the 45° angle later.

Do not stretch the strips when sewing. Stretching could cause the combinations to curve.

To get more accuracy and speed when ironing, I finger press first, scratching the fabric with my nail of the pointer finger along the seam line pushing the fabric in the direction that I want it to go. This will also avoid some of those pleats we don't want. Iron the seams of combination 1 down and Combination 2 up.

**Notice that combination 1 and combination 2 are sewn together at a different angle to achieve the star flower design later.**

Sew 5 sets of Combination 1 and 5 sets of Combination 2

Step #2

Fabric #1 is 2" wide
Fabric #2 is 1 1/2" wide
Fabric #3 is 1 1/2" wide
Fabric #4 is 1 1/2" wide
Fabric #5 is 1 1/2" wide
Fabric #6 is 2" wide

Fabric #1 is 2" wide
Fabric #2 is 1 1/2" wide
Fabric #3 is 1 1/2" wide
Fabric #4 is 1 1/2" wide
Fabric #5 is 1 1/2" wide
Fabric #6 is 2" wide

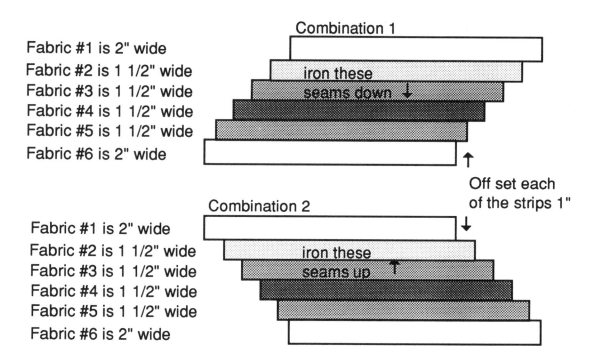

**Sewing check!** The six strips after sewn and ironed should measure between 5 1/2" to 5 5/8" wide.

## CUTTING STRIPS AT 45°

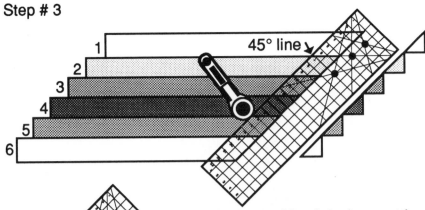

**Step #3.** Place the ruler on the sewn strips and line up the 45° line of the ruler parallel with one of the seam lines (center seams are best). Trim off the uneven edges. Move the ruler in 2" and cut a strip.

**Step # 3**

**Step # 4**

Step #4. Check before cutting each strip to see if the 45° angle on the ruler always lines up right. If not, you will have to trim off to make it right.

You will get 13 - 2" strips from each combination. You will need 60 strips from Combination 1 and 60 strips from Combination 2 for this quilt.

## SEWING THE FEATHERS

Step #5. Place one strip from Combination 1 and one from combination 2, right sides together. On one side the seams will be ironed up and on the other side the seam will be ironed down, which makes them lock together when sewn. You will be able to feel the seams match up with your fingers making it possible to finger pin as you sew these seams. Caution! If you sew too deep a seam, template R will not fit on them. Before you sew all of them together, iron open the seams on one block and check to see if template R will fit on top. If template R did fit the test block, chain sew the rest of these together.

Look at step #8 on page 23 to prepare template R.

Step #6. Place the template on the twelve patch and match up the horizontal score line with the middle seam and the vertical score line with the center seam indicated by the arrow. Cut around it with the Rotary Cutter. It is much easier to turn your work if you cut on a 9" x 12" Matt Board Base for this step.

Look at steps 10 - 16 on page 24 to see how to finish this quilt.

**Step #5**

Combination 1    2

**Step 6**

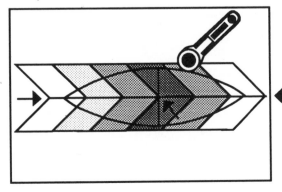

**28**

# STAR FLOWER

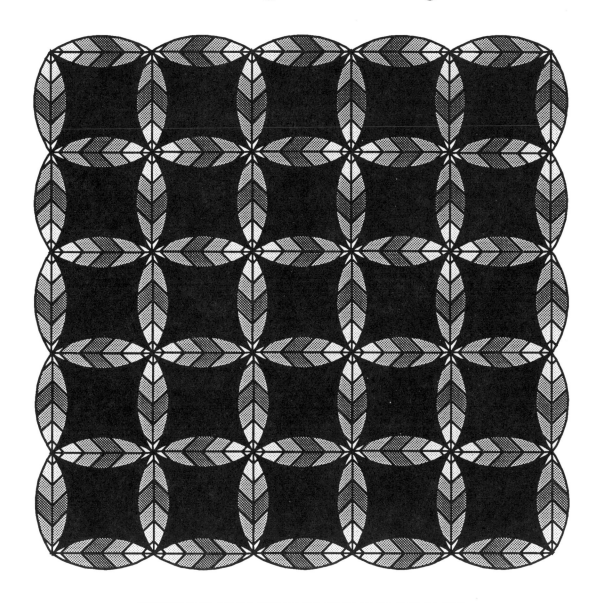

**FINISHED SIZE OF THIS QUILT IS 46" X 46"**
**IT IS PICTURED IN THE COLORED SECTION OF THIS BOOK**
## YARDAGE REQUIREMENTS:
Fabric #1 - 2/3 yd.
Fabric #2 - 1/2 yd.
Fabric #3 - 1/2 yd.
Fabric #4 - 1/2 yd.
Fabric #5 - 1/2 yd.
Fabric #6 - 2/3 yd.
Background fabric 2 yds.
Binding and back of quilt 2 2/3 yd. This fabric could be the same as the background fabric.

# CLOVER ALL OVER.

## Supplies Needed:
*E template from QS1
*Add On template R from QS2
*IBC Glass Head pins #5003
*Large Matt Board Cutting Base
*Small Matt Board Cutting Base
* 12" x 24" Omnigrid Ruler
*Small Rotary Cutter is best
*General Sewing Supplies

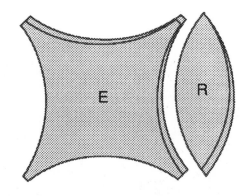

**READ PAGES 3 - 4 BEFORE STARTING THE QUILT.**

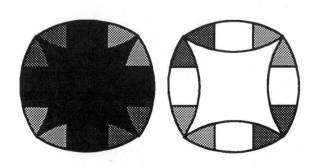

## CHOOSING THE FABRIC
When choosing fabrics for this quilt I like to first choose the background fabric and from it I pick the one or two colors that are going to be the four leaf clovers. If you choose only one fabric for the clovers of course every one will be the same color and if you choose two colors every other one will be a different color. You can also change the design dramatically by using a light or dark background. Look at the outside edge of the diagram on page 32 and notice that this design creates it's own unique border. You might want to experiment with a third color to form a stronger border.

I named this quilt after the Four Leaf Clovers that you are sometimes lucky enough to find when out for a walk. It would be a great gift for a Irish friend.

## CUTTING STRIPS FOR THE FOUR LEAF CLOVERS
## THE FINISHED SIZE OF THIS QUILT WILL BE 66" X 75"

In this pattern we will use 3 1/2" strips of two different fabrics for the Four Leaf Clovers and strips 4" wide for the center of the melon (the same as the background fabric). To change the size of the Four Leaf Clovers you would have to change the width of the strips cut from #1 and #2 fabrics.

To save time straighten and cut the strips from the two Four Leaf Clover fabrics at the same time because they are cut the same width. Make sure that the selvage edges match on each of them after they are folded in half. Look at pages 4 & 5 for straightening and cutting instructions.

## NUMBER OF STRIPS TO CUT FOR MELONS AND
## E'S TO CUT FOR BACKGROUND
Fabric 1 cut  10 - 3 1/2" strips
Fabric 2 cut  10 - 3 1/2" strips
Fabric 3 cut  10 - 4" strips
Cut 56 E's  (Look at step 1 on page 31 before cutting these.)

#1

#3

#2

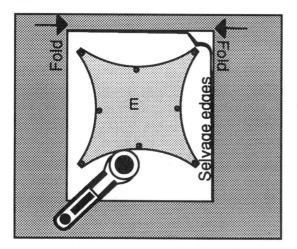

Step #1. Fold the fabric in half and in half again. Place template E on top and cut around it with the small Rotary Cutter. Make sure you have plenty of room to turn the board as you cut around the template. You will get 4 each time. Cut 56 E's.

**SEW THE STRIPS TOGETHER**

Step #2. Sew 10 sets of strips together using a scant 1/4" seam allowance. Sew the strips together following the order shown in diagram #4.

To get more accuracy and speed when ironing I Finger press the seams first, scratching the fabric with the nail of my pointer finger along the seam line pushing the fabric in the direction that I want it to go. This will avoid some of the pleats that we don't want. Press the seams towards the dark fabrics.

Step #3. Mark the template with two parallel lines 3 1/2" apart in the center by scoring it with a sharp object or marking pen.

Step #4. Place template R on top of the sewn strips lining up the scored lines with the seam lines. Cut around it with the Rotary Cutter. It is much easier to turn your work if you cut on a 9" x 12" Matt Board Base for this step.

You will get 13 melons from each set of sewn strips.

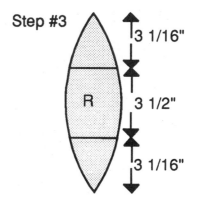

Step #3

3 1/16"

3 1/2"

3 1/16"

Step # 4

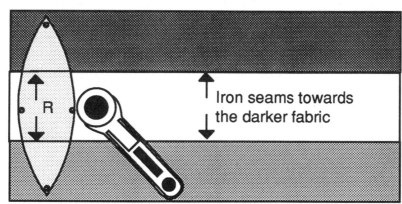

Iron seams towards the darker fabric

Fabric # 1 is 3 1/4" wide after it is sewn.

Fabric #3 is 3 1/2" wide after it is sewn

Fabric # 2 is 3 1/4" wide after it is sewn.

Cut 127 melons.

Step #5. Look at steps 10 - 16 on page 24 to see how to finish this quilt. Keep in mind that you can make this quilt as big or little as you want.

# CLOVER ALL OVER

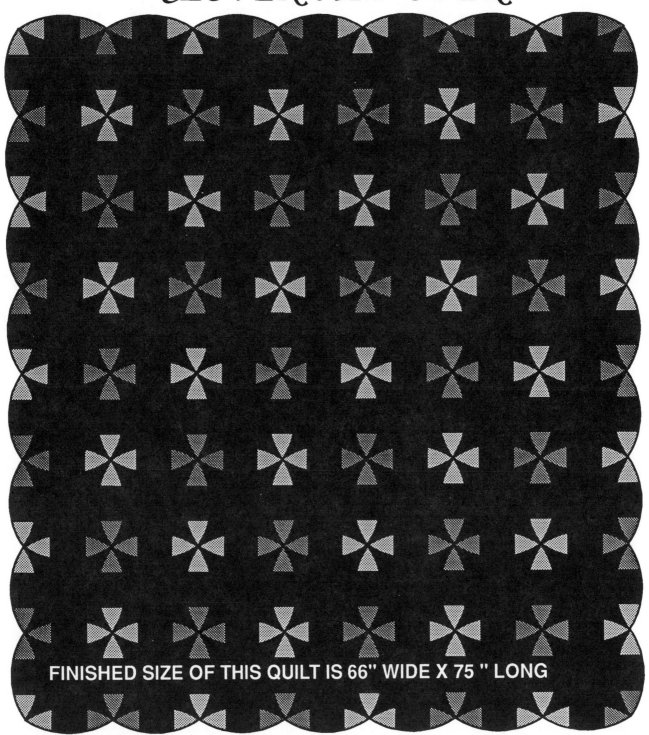

**FINISHED SIZE OF THIS QUILT IS 66" WIDE X 75 " LONG**

## YARDAGE REQUIREMENTS:

1 1/4 yd. fabric #1

1 1/4 yd. fabric #2

1 1/4 yd. fabric #3 - 1 1/4 yd. (This is the same color as the background fabric for the E's)

4 yd. Background fabric for E's (this is the same color as #3 fabric)

4 yds. for the back and 1 1/2 yds. for binding  (this could also be the same as #3 fabric)

# PATCHWORK PINES

## Supplies Needed:
*M, N, & O template from Pandora's Box
*Rotary Cutter
*Matt Board Cutting Base
*IBC Glass Head Pins #5003
*Fabric Grips

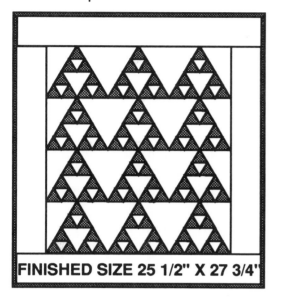

**FINISHED SIZE 25 1/2" X 27 3/4"**

### READ PAGES 3 - 4 BEFORE STARTING
### THE WALL QUILT
### CHOOSING THE FABRIC

Fabrics available with several scenes in them are great for this design because you can see through the templates when cutting making it possible to center a scene in the triangle. You waste fabric doing this, but the results make the waste worth while. I have also made this quilt using plaids and stripes and it is one of my favorite quilts. I did not pay attention to the grain line of the fabrics and it looked like an antique quilt when finished. The main thing you want to keep in mind is that you need a contrast in color and print. You could also use scraps and make each tree a different color.

## HOW THE TEMPLATES WORK TOGETHER

Before you start to cut I want to share with you how the 4 - 60° triangles from Pandora's Box work together.

They include the 1/4" seam allowance, and interchange with each other to create 100's of designs. They will also give you the ability to make miniature quilts, wall quilts and bed size quilts.

When sewn together
4 M's = 1 N
4 N's = 1 O
4 O's = 1 P

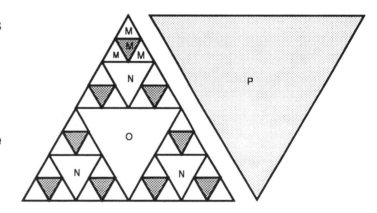

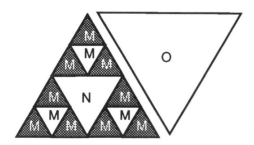

For the quilt in this pattern we will be using only the M, N and O templates.

The diagram to the left shows how we will be using the two colors in the wall quilt.

**33**

## NUMBER OF STRIPS TO CUT

Look at the instructions on pages 3 and 4 to see how to straighten the fabric and cut the strips.

- ☐ Cut 1 - 2" strip for the light M's
- ▨ Cut 3 - 2" strips for the dark M's
- ☐ Cut 1 - 3 1/4" strip for the light N's
- ☐ Cut 2 - 5 3/4" strip for the light O's

## NUMBER OF PIECES NEEDED

108 dark M's

36 light M's

12 light N's

16 light O's

## CUTTING THE TRIANGLES NEEDED

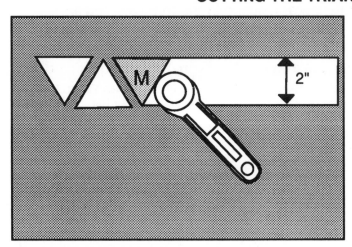

Look at the chart above to see how many of each triangle is needed and cut them. Layer the 2" strip of the light fabric and the 3- 2" strips of the dark fabric on top of each other. Be careful that all the edges of the strips line up with each other before cutting the triangles. If you have cut these strips at the same time it is easier because you won't have to line them up. Flip flop the template to save fabric while cutting, and continue to cut triangles until you have cut the number needed. Turn your cutting matt, not the fabric as you cut.

Next cut the N's from the 3 1/4" strip of the light fabric and the O's from the 5 3/4" strips of light fabric.

## SEWING TEST

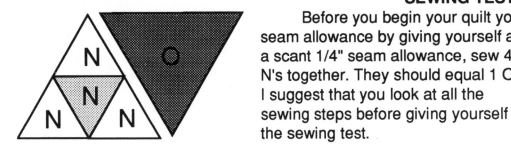

Before you begin your quilt you should test your seam allowance by giving yourself a sewing test. Using a scant 1/4" seam allowance, sew 4 N's together. They should equal 1 O. I suggest that you look at all the sewing steps before giving yourself the sewing test.

Step #1

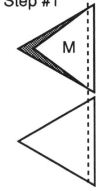

## SEWING STEPS

Step #1. After you have found the correct seam allowance you can begin to chain sew the pieces together saving time and thread. Place a light M and dark M right sides together with one of the edges being a straight edge and one edge being a bias edge. Try to do this without using pins to save time. Chain sew the M's together until you have 36 sets. This will be enough for all 12 trees in this quilt.

**Step #2**

Step #2. Clip the threads between all 36 sets. Finger press first, then iron the seams away from the center light triangle.

Step #3. Chain sew when adding the second dark triangle working your way around the center light triangle. Making this block is similar to making the Log Cabin because you are working around the center.

**Step #3**

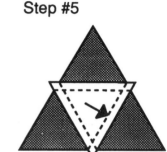

The only difference is that you are now working with triangles instead of squares and strips.

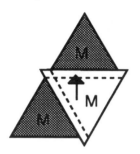

**Step #4**

Step #4. Clip the threads from the chain sewing and iron the seams of second triangle away from the center light triangle.

Step #5. Chain sew the third dark triangle to all 36 groups . You only need to finger pin the pieces together before sewing.

**Step #5**

Clip the threads between all the groups and iron the seams away from the center light triangle.

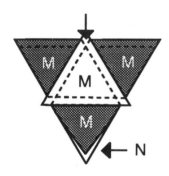

**Step #6**

Step # 6. With right sides to-gether place the M's on top of an N so you can see where the seams of the M's intersect when sewing. You do not have to pin them together before you sew this seam. Sew directly over the point the seams of the M intersect. Chain sew 12 of these. If you are using a fabric that has a scene in it you will have to be sure that the scene is facing in the right direction.

Step #7 Clip the threads be-tween all 12 and iron this seam allowance towards the M's, away from the N which will now become the center of the tree block.

**Step #7**

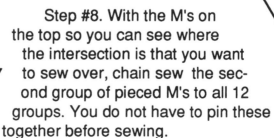

**Step #8**

Step #8. With the M's on the top so you can see where the intersection is that you want to sew over, chain sew the sec-ond group of pieced M's to all 12 groups. You do not have to pin these together before sewing.

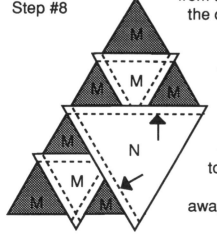

Clip all of the threads and iron this seam allowance away from the center N.

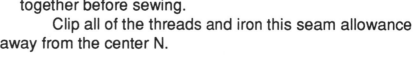

Step #9

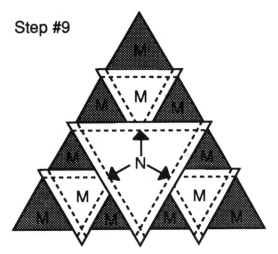

Step #9. Add the third group of M's to complete the tree.

You should now have 12 trees.

Finger press, then iron this seam away from the center N.

Step #10. If your seam allowance is correct the tree in step #9 should fit the O piece.

With right sides together and the tree on top of the O piece, the intersections will be visible that you want to sew over.

Step #10

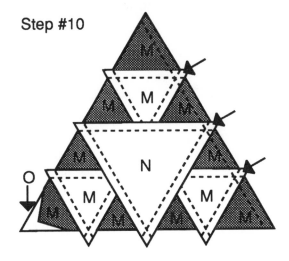

If the O piece has a scene in it, be sure it is sitting in the right direction.

Finger pin and sew this seam, sewing directly over each intersection.

Press the seam allowance towards the O piece.

Step #11. Keep adding the trees to the O's until you have 3 trees and 4 O pieces in each row.

Make four rows

Step #11 & 12

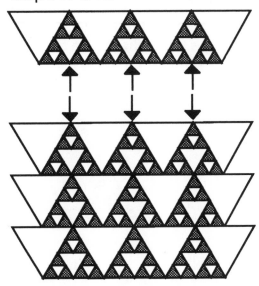

Step # 13. Place a ruler along the edge of the quilt and trim off the triangle excess using the Rotary Cutter. **Caution!** Do not trim off the 1/4" seam allowance along the outside edge.

Step # 12. This is the first time that you will need to use pins in the construction of this quilt. Insert the pin at the intersection of the top and second row exactly where the seams intersect. Sew with row one on top because it has more intersections over which to sew. Continue to add the other two rows in the same way.

Step #13

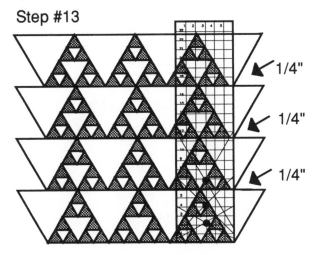

1/4"

1/4"

1/4"

Step # 14. Cut 4 strips for the borders 4 1/4" wide.

Measure the length of both sides and take the average measurement. Cut the borders strips to the length of the average measurement. If you start to sew the borders on without cutting them the same lengths first, the edges of the quilt will have a chance of being ruffled.

Attach the side borders first  and sew these seams with the border strips on the bottom so the seam intersections that you want to sew over are visible. Press these seams towards the outside edge.

Measure the top and bottom edges after the side borders have been added and take the average measurement. Cut the top and bottom borders the length of the average measurement.

Next attach the top and bottom borders.

**FINISHED SIZE OF THIS QUILT IS 25 1/2" X 27 3/4"**

## YARDAGE REQUIREMENTS:

1 1/2 yd. of light fabric for M's, N's, O's, borders and backs
    1/2 yd. of dark fabric for M's and binding

# FLYING GEESE

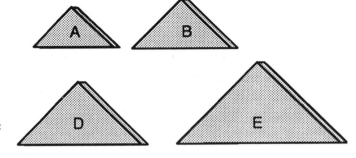

## Supplies Needed:
*Templates  A & B, B & D, or D & E from
Pandora's Box
*Matt Board cutting Base
*Rotary Cutter
*Omnigrid Ruler 6" x 24"
*Chaco- liner or chalk pencil to mark fabric
*IBC Glass Head Pins #5003

## READ PAGES 3 & 4 BEFORE STARTING

### CHOOSING THE FABRIC
For this quilt you will use a stripe cut from a border print fabric between each of the rows of Flying Geese. First choose this fabric. This fabric may have stripes of different widths. Use the widest stripe for the outside border of the quilt and a narrower one for connecting the rows of geese.

The width of the stripe will help you to determine which size you want to make the geese. For example you do not want to use a small Flying Geese block with a wide border print.

You will want to pick fabrics that go with your border print  for the geese and the sky in the block. You may use many colors for the geese and only one lighter fabric for the sky; or the sky could be many different colors. Be sure that the sky is lighter than the geese so the fabrics in the block don't mush together like the top example of step #1.

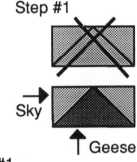

Step #1

Sky

Geese

Step # 2

2" wide
finished size

3" wide
finished size

4" wide
finished size

Step #2. There are three sizes of geese to choose from in Pandora's Box.

The length of the quilt is determined by the length that you cut the border strips and the width is determined by the number of rows of geese and border strips used. The size of the Flying Geese block and the width of the border strips will also make a difference in the finished size.

### THE FLYING GEESE BLOCK
Step #3. For this quilt we are going to be working with template D and E.  Notice in diagram #3 that the bias in each block is in the center of the block. You will have many problems later keeping the geese flying straight if the bias ends up on the outside edge of the block; the fabric would want to stretch when sewing the geese to the border strips.

Step # 3

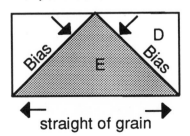

straight of grain

# CUTTING THE GEESE

Look at pages 3 & 4 to see how to straighten the fabric and cut strips for the geese.
I used 12 different reds and greens for the geese and a neutral color for the sky.

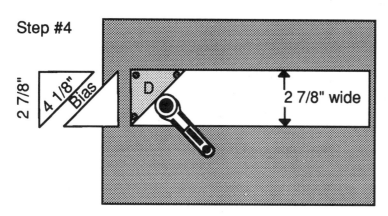

Step #4

Step #4. To cut the sky piece layer as many as 6- 2 7/8" strips on top of each other. Make sure that the edges of the strips are lined up. Place template D on top of the strips just inside the selvage edge and make sure that the bias will end up in the center of the block. Flip flop the template each time you cut a new set of pieces with the Rotary Cutter and continue across the strip until it is all used up. You will not waste any fabric cutting the pieces this way.

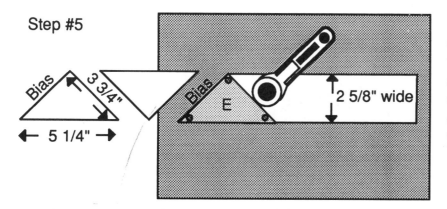

Step #5

Step #5. To cut the geese, place template E on top of 6 layers of 2 5/8" strips. Flip flop the template each time you cut a new set of pieces and continue until you have used up the strips.

## CUTTING THE BORDER STRIPS

Step #6. A lot of the border prints will have more than one stripe that you can use. After you have decided which ones you want to use, cut the strip. Place the ruler 1/4" from where you want the seam line to fall and cut with a Rotary Cutter. I have indicated by arrows where it should be cut apart. The length of the border strips plus the width of the top and bottom border will determine the length of the quilt.

Step #6

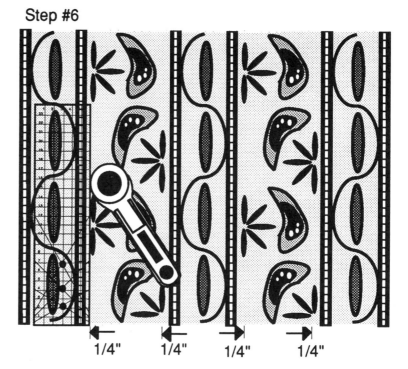

1/4"    1/4"    1/4"    1/4"

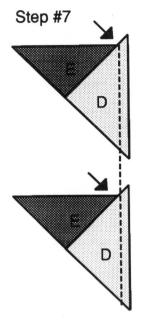

Step #7

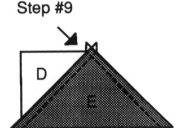

Step #7. With right sides together place a D piece (sky) on top of the E matching up the bottom edges. The D piece will extend above the E at the top because the 1/4" seam allowance is included. Finger pin while sewing these pieces together. Chain sew many sets of these with a scant 1/4" seam allowance.

Step #8. First finger press the seam towards the D (sky), then press with an iron.

Step #9. With right sides together add the second D. Match up the bottom edges and on the top there will be a tail allowing for the 1/4". Finger pin and guide the pieces with your fingers as you sew many blocks.

Step #10. First finger press, then iron this seam towards the D. On the center top and on each bottom corner there will be tails.

Step #11. This diagram shows how the block should look on the right side after it has been pressed. There should be a 1/4" seam allowance from the arrow to the upper edge.

Step #8

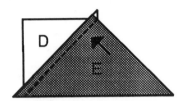

Step #9

Step #10

Step #11

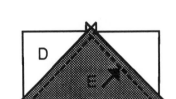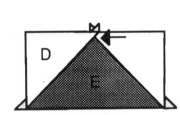

Step #12. After you have made all of the blocks that you need, lay them on a table (or on the floor if you need more room) and arrange them the way you want them to be in the quilt. Make sure that blocks alike are not next to each other going across or up and down. Give each row a #.

Step #13. Stack the blocks one on top of the other with the top block on the bottom of the pile. Continue stacking until the bottom block is on top.

Step #12

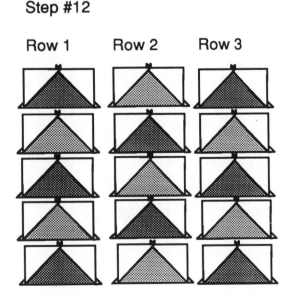

Step #13

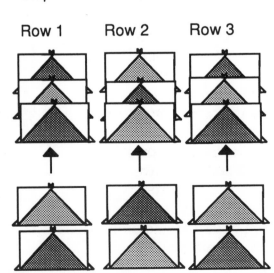

40

Step #14

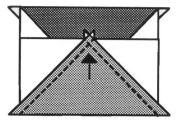

Step #14. Make sure the piles are in the right order when you start to sew. Take the two top blocks in Row 1 and place them right sides together. Sew with the block on top that has the seam intersection (indicated by the arrow) in the middle so you can see exactly the point over which you want to sew.

Step #15. Connect the blocks together now into vertical strips by chain sewing **directly over the seam intersections** indicated by the arrows for perfect corners. Finger pin to save time when sewing these together. **Do not cut the threads between the blocks**. Continue until all of the rows are connected.

Step #15

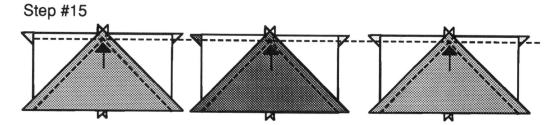

## MARK THE CHALK LINES ON THE BORDER STRIPS

Step #16. Line up the cut border print strips touching each other. Make sure that the same design in the border print is always matched up horizontally. Connect them to each other with small pieces of masking tape. To get the distance you need between each chalk line, measure the distance between the seam lines of the connected blocks from step 15. When using templates D & E it should be 2" from seam line to seam line. The two outside border print strips should be cut longer to allow for the mitered corner on the outside border. Mark the border print strips with a chacoliner or fabric chalk pencil 2" apart **except for the top and bottom ones which will have to be 2 1/4"** to allow for the 1/4" seam allowance.

Step #16

Outside border strips should be cut longer to allow for the mitered corners.

2 1/4"
2"
2"
2"

2 1/4"

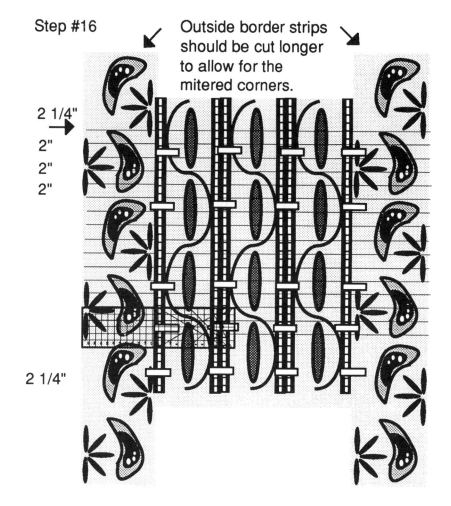

41

## CONNECTING THE GEESE TO THE BORDER STRIPS

Step #17. Cut one of the strips of geese from step #17. Iron as shown in the diagram. With the geese on top match up each horizontal chalk line on the border strips to each intersection (indicated by the arrows) of the Flying Geese block and insert a pin. Sew this seam with the geese on top, sewing directly over the seam intersections indicated by the arrows. If you keep matching up the chalk lines to each seam line, the geese will be flying straight in the finished quilt.

Step #18. Keep adding more rows of geese and border strips until you have the center part of the quilt as wide as you want.

Iron these seams towards the border strips.

Measure the distance from the top to the bottom of the quilt and take the average length of the two sides. Subtract the 1/4" from the top and bottom. To this measurement you have to add the amount needed for the mitered corner. To find the amount of extra length needed fold the strip of border print you are going to use for the outside border in half on the diagonal and place a mark where the fold ended. Allow a bit extra past the fold when cutting it off. It is important that the length of border added to both sides is exactly the same. If it is not, the quilt will not hang straight.

When adding the outside border, sew with the geese on top. Stop sewing 1/4" from each corner on the top and bottom of the quilt.

Step #19. After the side borders are on, sew the borders on the top and bottom of the quilt. Repeat the same steps from Step #18 to find the length needed. Again allow enough length for the mitered corners. Stop sewing 1/4" from each end on these seams. **Do not sew past the corners.** The seam lines should touch in each of the four corners.

**Step #17**

Iron

2 1/4"

2"

2"

2"

2 1/4"

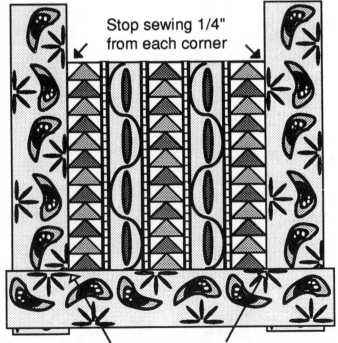

**Step #18**

Stop sewing 1/4"
from each corner

Step #19  Stop sewing 1/4" from each corner

42

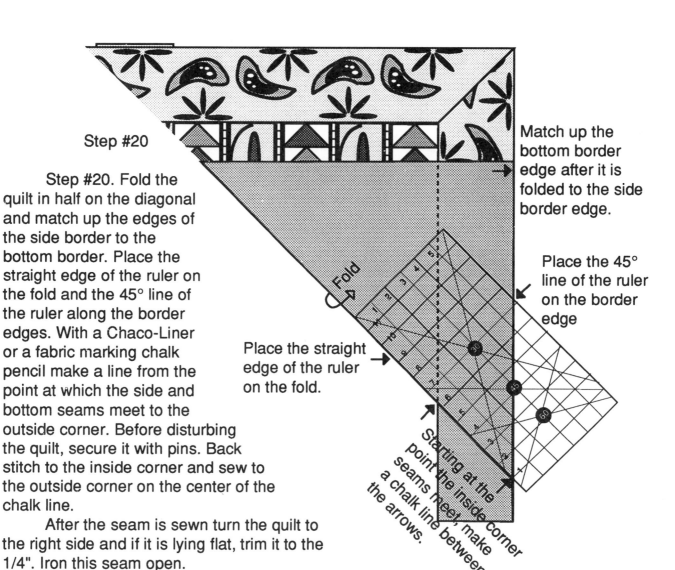

Match up the bottom border edge after it is folded to the side border edge.

Place the 45° line of the ruler on the border edge

Place the straight edge of the ruler on the fold.

Fold

Starting at the point the inside corner seams meet, make a chalk line between the arrows.

Step #20

Step #20. Fold the quilt in half on the diagonal and match up the edges of the side border to the bottom border. Place the straight edge of the ruler on the fold and the 45° line of the ruler along the border edges. With a Chaco-Liner or a fabric marking chalk pencil make a line from the point at which the side and bottom seams meet to the outside corner. Before disturbing the quilt, secure it with pins. Back stitch to the inside corner and sew to the outside corner on the center of the chalk line.

After the seam is sewn turn the quilt to the right side and if it is lying flat, trim it to the 1/4". Iron this seam open.

Repeat this step on all four corners.

### YARDAGE
I did not give the yardage for this quilt because there are so many factors that effect the finished size. I suggest that you first buy the border print the length that you want the quilt. If you are making a bed size quilt you will need two 3 yd. lengths of border print. Then choose the fabrics for the geese and the sky.

43

# INNER CITY

## Supplies Needed:
* templates J, H, L, & N from Pandora's Box (QS 15)
* Fabric Grips
* Rotary Cutter
* Large Matt Board Cutting Base
* IBC Glass Head Pins #5003 1 3/8" long
* 6" x 24" Omnigrid Ruler

**READ PAGES 3 - 4 & 44 - 48 BEFORE STARTING**

### SELECTION OF FABRICS FOR INNER CITY
For this quilt it is important to select three fabrics of 100% cotton with a high contrast ranging from light to dark. These fabrics should also have a variety of print and background so that the pieces don't appear to mush together in the quilt.

### NUMBER OF STRIPS TO CUT FOR THE INNER CITY

■ **From the darkest fabric:**
Cut 3 strips 3" wide for the combination blocks 2,3, & 4
Cut 4 strips 3" wide for the border
Cut 1 strip 3 1/4" wide for template N
Cut 4 strips 2" wide for bindings
Cut 1 strip 2" wide for the template L

▨ **From the medium colored fabric:**
Cut 1 strip 3 1/4" wide for template N
Cut 1 strip 2" wide for template L
Cut 4 strips 3" wide for the combination blocks 1, 3, & 4

▢ **From the lightest fabric:**
Cut 1 strip 2" wide for template L
Cut 1 strip 3 1/4" wide for template N
Cut 4 strips 3" wide for the combination blocks 1,2, & 4

### SEWING TEST
Step #1. Before you sew all of the combination strips together give yourself a sewing test. Sew one combination of strips from step #2 with a scant 1/4" seam allowance about 8" and check to see that template J will fit OK on the strips after they are sewn as it shows in the diagram to the right. If it isn't a fit, correct the seam allowance before you sew the rest of the combination strips together. If the strips are wider than the template after they are sewn you can trim them off.

Step #1

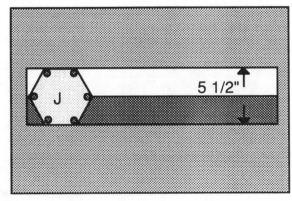

5 1/2"

Step #2.
Sew a 3" light and a 3" medium strip together for combination 1. Sew **two** sets of combination 1.

Sew a 3" light and a 3" dark strip together for combination 2. Sew **one** of these.

Sew a 3" medium and a 3" dark strip together for combination 3. Sew **one** of these.

Ironing the seams **open** on all of the combinations will make cutting the blocks out easier in step #3.

Step #2

Combination 1

Combination 2

Combination 3

## CUTTING THE BLOCK COMBINATIONS

Step #3

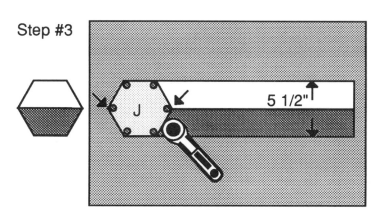

Step #3 Place the J template on one of the sewn combination strips. Line up the points of the template on the seam line. **Cut only one at a time** because it would be impossible to line up the seam lines perfectly on more than one of the sewn strips.

Continue this step until you have cut the blocks needed for combination one, two and three. Look at the diagram below to see how many to cut.

Cut 8 blocks from the combination 1 strips

 Cut 6 blocks from the combination 2 strips

Cut 6 blocks from the combination 3 strips

## CUTTING THE DIAMONDS

Step #4

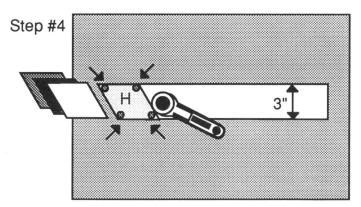

Step #4. To cut the diamonds for template H stack one of each of the light, medium, and dark 3" cut strips on top of each other. Make sure that the edges of the strips are in line. Place template H on top and cut out with the Rotary Cutter.

Cut 9 diamonds of each color.

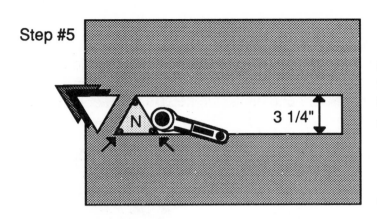

**Step #5**

## CUTTING TRIANGLES

Step #5. Stack a 3 1/4" strip of each of the light, medium and dark fabrics on top of each other. Place template N on top of the cut strips and cut the triangles with the Rotary Cutter. Flip flop the template to save fabric.

You will need 1 light, 1 medium and 4 dark triangles.

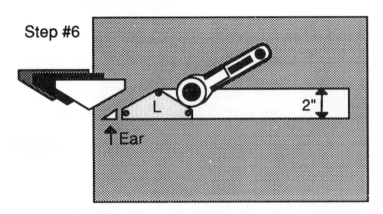

**Step #6**

## CUTTING ISOSCELES TRIANGLES

Step #6. Stack a 2" strip of each of the light, medium and dark fabrics on top of each other. Place template L on top and cut the triangles with the Rotary Cutter. Cut the ears off last.

You will need 3 light, 3 medium, and 3 dark L's.

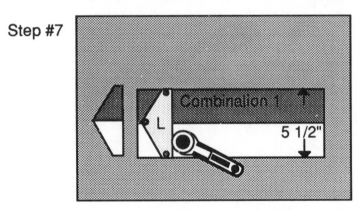

**Step #7**

Step #7. To get the split isosceles triangles used in row 8, (look on page 47 at Step #14) place the L template on the left over sewn combination 1 strips. You will need 2 of these.

## SEWING THE BABY BLOCK

Step #8. To help keep the pieces of the Baby Block in the right position while working at the sewing machine, lay the light, medium, and dark cut diamonds right side up as shown in the diagram to the right.

**Step #8**

**Step #9**

Read the instructions for steps #9 - #11 before continuing.

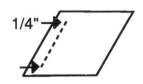

Step #9. With right sides together, and using a scant 1/4" seam allowance, sew a light and medium diamond together. Back stitch to **1/4" from each end.**

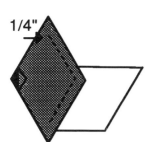

1/4"

Step #10. Always put the third piece you're adding on the bottom so the first seam you made will be visible making it easy to know where to stop sewing. In this block the dark diamond is on the bottom right side facing up. Back stitch **to 1/4" from the outside edge** then sew to the middle and back stitch at the intersection that the seams connect.

Step #11

Step #11. To sew the last seam of the Baby Block, start sewing from the outside edge and work to the inside of the block. Back stitch on both ends of this seam.

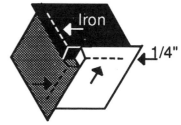

Iron the seams to one side in a circular motion. If the block has been sewn right it will lie flat.

## SEWING TEST

Give yourself a sewing test by checking to see if these three pieces sewn together fit the J template. If not, you need to adjust to the scant 1/4" seam allowance.

Step #12

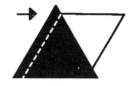

Step #12. Look at Step #14 and you will see that rows 3, 5, and 7 end up with diamond and triangle combinations. Sew them together to fill out these rows. There will be a tail at the top of the triangles when sewing them together.

Step #14

Step #13

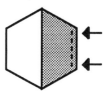

Step #13. Because the seams connecting the pieces in rows 1 & 8 would be so short, it is easier to sew each of these pieces in separately. The first and last piece in row one is trimmed off after it is sewn on. For rows 2 - 7, sew the blocks together to form the rows as shown. Back stitch 1/4" from the beginning and end of each seam.

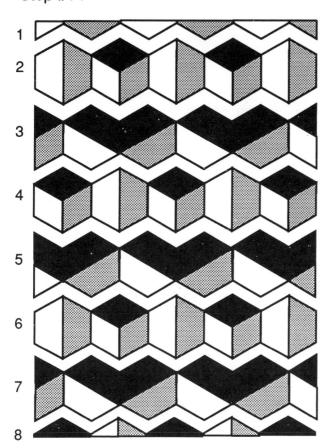

1
2
3
4
5
6
7
8

Step #14. Next, sew the rows together. Instead of pivoting at each corner treat each seam as a separate one. Back stitch at the end of each seam.

It is easier to iron the seams after adding each row.

47

## ATTACH THE BORDERS

Before attaching the borders, make sure that the corners are square. You can check this by placing a square ruler on the corners and trim if needed.

Look at Steps #18 - #20 on pages 42 and 43 to see how to attach borders with mitered corners.

Caution! Be sure the opposite borders are cut the same length. If they aren't you take a chance on the edge of the quilt being ruffled.

Press all seams.

# *INNER CITY*

**FINISHED SIZE OF THIS QUILT IS 30" X 32"**
**YARDAGE REQUIREMENTS:**

2 1/4 yd. dark        (this will be enough for the back and binding too.)
3/4 yd. of medium
3/4 yd. of light

---

If you want to make this quilt in the miniature size (15" x 18") from Pandora's Box use templates I, K, M, and G.

**FINISHED SIZE 15" X 18"**
**YARDAGE REQUIREMENTS:**
1 yd. dark (this will be enough for the back and binding too)
1/3 yd. of medium
1/3 yd. of light

Top Left: This Double wedding Ring made in 1992 was designed by Sharlene Jorgenson, pieced by Phyllis Petersen, and hand quilted by Esther Grischowsky. Instructions start on page 5.

Top right: This Glorified Nine Patch made in1992 was designed by Sharlene Jorgenson, pieced by Phyllis Petersen and Sharlene Jorgenson, and machine quilted by Dalene Thomas. Instructions start on page 15.

Bottom left: This Diamond Double Wedding Ring made in 1991 was designed by Sharlene Jorgenson, pieced by Sharlene Jorgenson and Phyllis Petersen and machine quilted by Julie Borge. Instructions start on page 21.

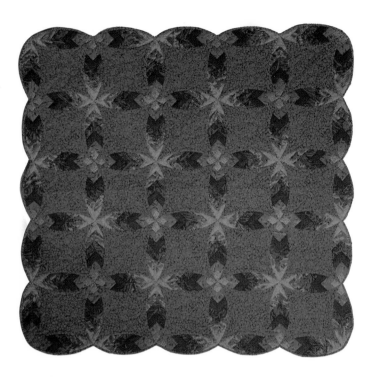

Top left: This Star Flower made in 1992 was designed by Sharlene Jorgenson, pieced and machine quilted by Phyllis Petersen. Instructions start on page 26.

Top right: This Clover All Over made in 1991 was designed by Sharlene Jorgenson, pieced by Phyllis Peterson and machine quilted by Julie Borge. Instructions start on page 30.

Bottom left: This Patchwork Pines wall quilt made in 1992 was designed by Sharlene Jorgenson, machine pieced and quilted by Phyllis Petersen. Instructions start on page 33.

Top left: The Flying Geese wall quilt made 1992 was designed by Sharlene Jorgenson, pieced and quilted by Phyllis Petersen. Instructions start on page 38.

Top right: The Inner City made in 1991 was designed and pieced by Sharlene Jorgenson, and machine quilted by Dalene Thomas. Instructions start on page 44.

Bottom left: The Chinese Checkers wall quilt made in 1992 was designed by Sharlene Jorgenson, pieced and quilted by Phyllis Petersen. Instructions start on page 53.

The Crazy Quilt wall hanging made in 1992 was designed and pieced by Sharlene Jorgenson. Instructions start on page 60.

The Bow Tie wall quilt made in 1992 was designed by Sharlene Jorgenson, machine pieced and quilted by Phyllis Petersen. Instructions on page 65.

The Kaleidescope table cloth made in 1992 was designed by Sharlene Jorgenson, machine pieced and quilted by Phyllis Petersen. Instructions start on page 69.

The Drunkard's Path wall quilt was designed by Sharlene Jorgenson pieced by Phyllis Petersen and machine quilted by Dalene Thomas. Instructions start on page 74.

# CHINESE CHECKERS

## Supplies Needed:
*Template H and M from Pandora's Box
*Large Matt Board Cutting Base
*Small 9" x 12" Matt Board Base (optional)
*Rotary Cutter
*6" x 24" Omnigrid Ruler
*IBC Glass Head Pins #5003

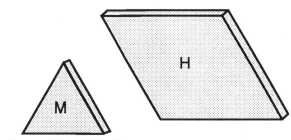

**READ PAGES 3 - 4 BEFORE STARTING**

### CHOOSING THE FABRICS FOR CHINESE CHECKERS

First choose the border print fabric that you want to outline the outside edge of the quilt. Then choose colors from the border print to use in the stars. There are 48 of the 60° triangles in each of the stars and because I used only two color families I needed 24 reds and 24 greens. I did not have that many of each of the colors so I used each of the fabrics twice in every star. It is much easier to choose the fabric for the background (diamonds) after some of the stars have been constructed.

The stars can also be made up from scraps left over from other quilting projects. You would just have to separate the light and dark fabrics and use equal amounts of each when constructing the stars. This quilt looks great made either way.

### NUMBER OF STRIPS TO CUT FROM NEW FABRIC
Cut 1 - 2" strips from 12 different reds
Cut 1 - 2" strips from 12 different greens
Cut 3 - 3" strips from the background (diamond) fabric

Step #1

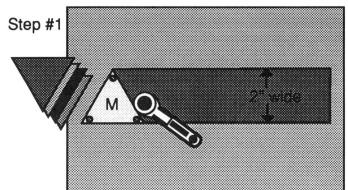

### CUTTING THE TRIANGLES

Step #1. Layer up to 6 of the 2" strips on top of each other. Make sure the edges are lined up straight. Place template M on top of the strips and cut along the edge of the template with the Rotary Cutter. Flip flop the template after you have cut each set of triangles and line up the template with the previous cut edge.

### CUTTING THE DIAMONDS

Step #2. Layer the 3 - 3" strips on top of each other. Make sure the edges are lined up straight. Place template H on top of the strips and cut along the edge of the template with the Rotary Cutter. Move the template over after each cut and line up with the first cut.

Step #2

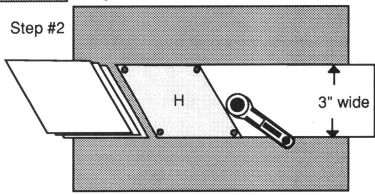

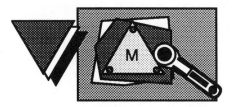

Step #3

## CUTTING FROM SCRAPS

You don't want to lose accuracy by disturbing the fabric and template when cutting, so it works best to cut scraps on a smaller (9" x 12") Matt Board Base giving you the ability to turn the board as you cut around the template.

You don't have to be concerned about the grain of the fabric when cutting out these small triangles.

You would need 180 light M's, and 180 dark M's from scraps.

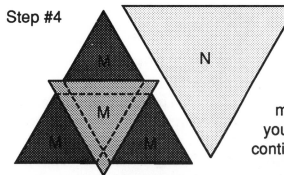

Step #4

## SEWING TEST

Step #4. Read Steps #5 - 9 before giving yourself this sewing test. Before you put the pedal to the metal and begin to chain sew you need to give yourself a sewing test. With a **scant 1/4" seam allowance** sew 4 M's together. They must equal the N from Pandora's Box. If they do not, you must adapt your seam allowance before you continue to make the Chinese Checkers.

## SEWING STEPS FOR THE TREE BLOCKS

Step #5

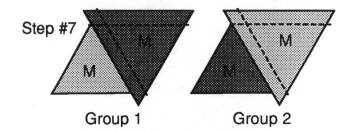

Step #5. After you have passed the sewing test you can start to chain sew the M's together. Place a red (light) and a green (dark) M right sides together with one having the straight edge and one the bias edge. Chain sew 12 sets. This is enough for one star. Do not back stitch as this would create bulk in the corners and you don't need to use pins until Step #10.

Now divide the pieces from Step #1 into two groups of six. On one group you will want to have a red (light) center when finished and on the other you want to have a green (dark) center.

Step #6

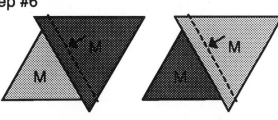

Step #6. On 6 of these, iron the seam away from the green (dark) center triangle and on the other 6 iron the seam away from the red (light) center triangle.

Step #7

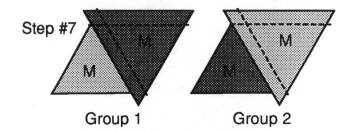

Group 1          Group 2

Step #8

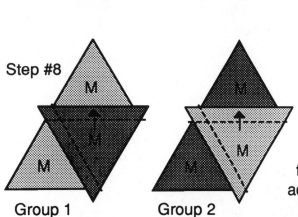

Group 1          Group 2

Step #7. Next, add the second red (light) triangle to group 1 and the second green (dark) triangle to group 2. Place the piece you are adding on the bottom and chain sew 6 of each.

Step #8. Always iron the seams away from the center triangles.

**54**

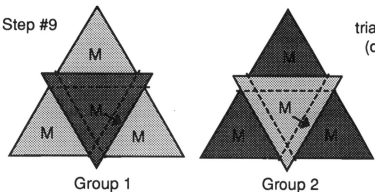

Step #9

Group 1          Group 2

Step #9. Add the third red (light) triangle to group 1 and the third green (dark) triangle to group 2.

Iron the seams away from the center.

You should now have 6 groups with a red (light) center and 6 groups with a green (dark) center.

Step #10. Place a group with a red (light) center and a group with a green (dark) center right sides together.

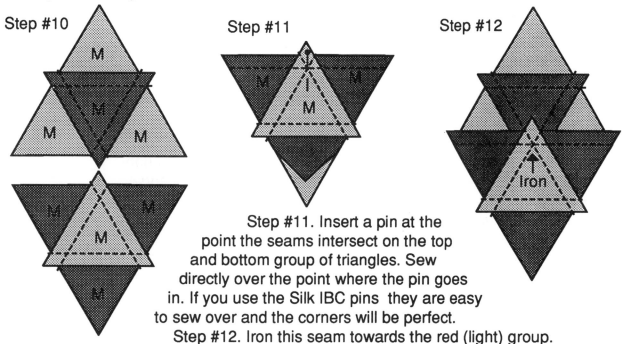

Step #10          Step #11          Step #12

Step #11. Insert a pin at the point the seams intersect on the top and bottom group of triangles. Sew directly over the point where the pin goes in. If you use the Silk IBC pins they are easy to sew over and the corners will be perfect.

Step #12. Iron this seam towards the red (light) group.

Step #13. Add the second group of red (light) triangles repeating Step #11 and iron this seam towards the red (light) group.

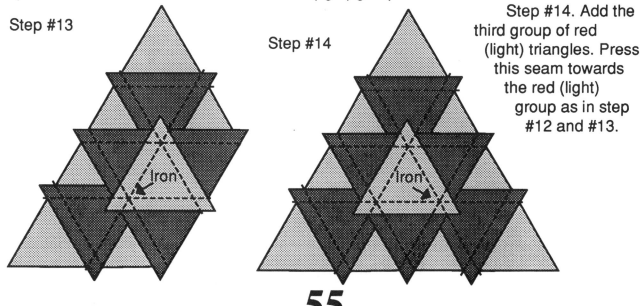

Step #13          Step #14

Step #14. Add the third group of red (light) triangles. Press this seam towards the red (light) group as in step #12 and #13.

**55**

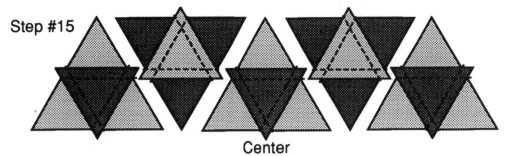

Step #15

Center

Step #15.
Arrange red (light)
and green (dark)
groups of triangles
as shown in the
diagram for the
bottom of the tree
block.

Step #16
Starting with the **center** group
of red (light) triangles of Step
#15 sew the triangles together.
Diagram #16 shows you in
which order to sew them. The
arrows with numbers indicate

Seam 3          Seam 4

Step #16

Seam 1        Seam 2

Step #17

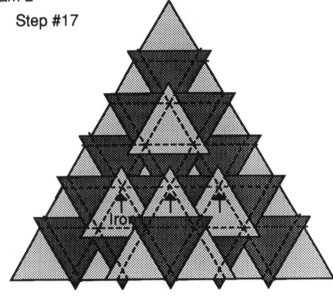

the order in which you sew the seams.
Press the seam in the direction indicated
by the arrow after each seam is sewn.

Step #17. To connect the top and
bottom of the tree block, insert a pin
through the top and bottom of the tree at
each intersection indicated by the arrows. Sew directly over the point the pin
goes in. Iron this seam up.

Make 7 of these tree blocks.

Step #18

Seam 2        Seam 1

H

Iron    Iron

H          H

Iron

Seam 3        Seam 4

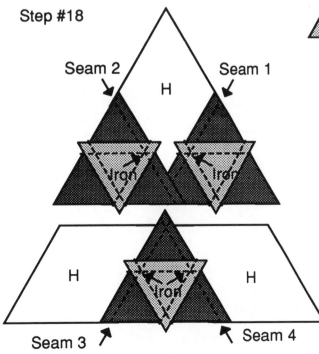

The two main blocks that make this
quilt resemble trees. You have just
finished the first one.

Step #18. The second tree block
that makes up the Chinese Checkers
quilt design has the H piece in it. Follow
the arrows and attach a set of green
(dark) triangles to a background H piece
until you have 2 parts of a block that look
just like the diagram.

Iron after each of the seams are
sewn. If you work on all 6 of these at one
time you can chain sew, saving time and
thread.

**56**

Step #19. Finish all six of these trees by connecting the top section to the bottom section.

Iron this seam down on all six trees.

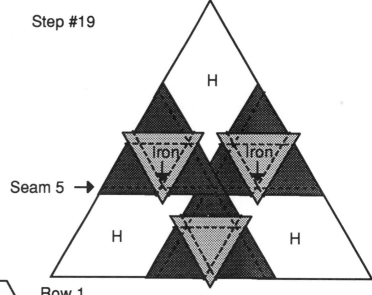

Step #19

Step #20. To make the blocks to complete the quilt, repeat Steps #5 - #9 and make 3 more groups with a red (light) center and 3 groups with a green (dark) center.

Step #20

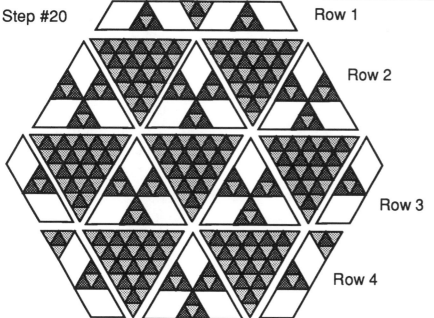

Row 1
Row 2
Row 3
Row 4

Lay out the tree blocks as shown in the diagram. You will need to make row 1 for the top of this quilt as pictured. Next make the end blocks for rows 3 and 4 and put them in place as shown in the diagram.

Step #21. Sew the blocks together into rows. Sew with the piece on top that has the most intersections to sew over, making it easier to finish with perfect points on the right side.

Step 21

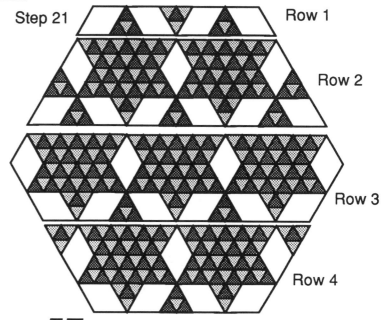

Row 1
Row 2
Row 3
Row 4

**57**

# ATTACHING THE BORDERS

**Step #22**

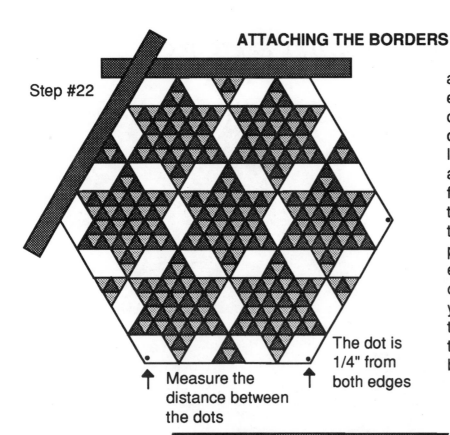

Measure the distance between the dots

The dot is 1/4" from both edges

Step #22. Put a dot on all six corners 1/4" from both edges. Measure the distance on all six sides between the dots and find the average length. To this measurement add the extra amount needed for the mitered corner. To find the extra amount needed, fold the strip at a 60° angle and place a mark where the fold ended. Allow a bit extra when cutting it off. It is important that you cut the six border strips all the same length. Attach them to the quilt between the dots, back stitching at both ends.

Step #22. Fold the quilt in half and match up the edges of the borders. Place the straight edge of the ruler on the fold and the 60° line of the ruler along the border edges. With a Chaco-Liner or a fabric marking chalk pencil make a line from the point the border seams meet to the outside corner.

Before disturbing the quilt secure it with pins. Sew this seam on the center of the chalk line. Back stitch to the inside corner and sew to the outside corner.

After these seams are sewn on all six corners, press these seams open. If the corners lie flat, trim the seams to 1/4".

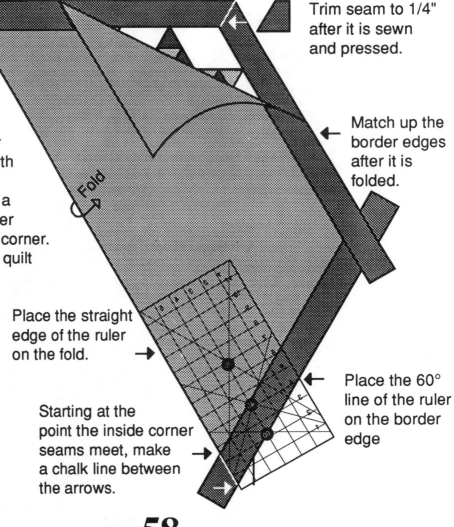

Trim seam to 1/4" after it is sewn and pressed.

Match up the border edges after it is folded.

Fold

Place the straight edge of the ruler on the fold.

Place the 60° line of the ruler on the border edge

Starting at the point the inside corner seams meet, make a chalk line between the arrows.

# CHINESE CHECKERS

**SHOWN IN COLOR ON PAGE 51**
**FINISHED SIZE: 33 1/2" (TOP TO BOTTOM)**
**YARDAGE REQUIREMENTS:**
1 - 2" strip of 12 different reds
1 - 2" strip of 12 different greens
3/4 yd. border print
1/2Yd. for background (diamonds)
1 1/4 yd. backing and binding

* You can also use scraps for the stars.

**COLOR YOUR OWN CHINESE CHECKERS DESIGN**

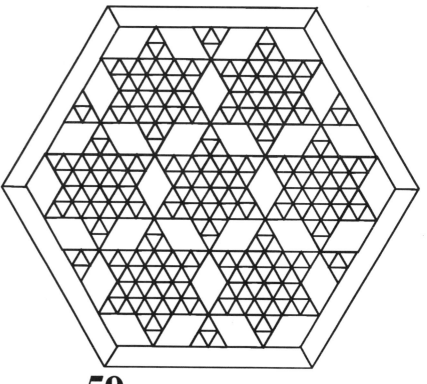

# CRAZY QUILT

## Supplies Needed:
*You can use either the 6" (#QS7) or
 12" (#QS6) Crazy Quilt Templates
*Large Matt Board Cutting Base
*9" x 12" Matt Board Cutting Base
*Rotary Cutter
*Fabric Grips
*6" x 24" Omnigrid Ruler (if using new fabric)

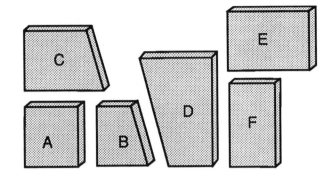

**READ PAGES 3 - 4 BEFORE STARTING THE QUILT**

### CHOOSING FABRICS FOR THE CRAZY QUILT

This quilt will give you a chance to recycle blue jeans, wool skirts, corduroys, velvets, or clean up the scraps left over from other sewing projects. Outdated neckties work up great into this design. You will want to sew with a walking foot when using ties because the fabric will tend to slip.

If you decide to use new yardage choose 8 different fabrics with a variety of background, print, and value so the pieces don't mush together.

This would be a great quilt to make for a child's room, college dorm, picnics and lake cabins. It is also a great way to make yardage for other garments like vests and jackets.

### TIPS NICE TO KNOW IF YOU ARE USING AN OVERLOCK MACHINE

You might want to embellish the cut denim pieces with left over laces, ribbons etc. before sewing them into the blocks; add buttons and other memorabilia after the quilt is finished. If you're using a four thread overlock machine and want the finished seams with a lot of color to end up on the right side, sew with the pieces **wrong** sides together instead of right sides together and use variegated thread in both the upper and lower looper and yellow in the right needle and green in the left needle. Also, the blocks will be more colorful if you use both the right and wrong sides of the blue jeans. I have also made this quilt mixing new fabric with the blue jeans and have been very pleased with the results. Let your imagination be your guide and have fun planning the quilt.

If you don't want to add batting and a back you don't have to because this quilt will be finished as you go as well as reversible and very durable.

To finish the outside edge of the quilt you can fold an 8" strip of fabric in half **wrong** sides together and add it to the edge with the overlock seam.

Progress will be a lot faster if you work on two blocks at one time because you will be able to clip the threads between each of the seams instead of chaining off after the addition of each piece.

Slow down when you approach the extra bulk in pieces with pockets so you don't break the needle or harm the serger; finger pinning is good enough when sewing the pieces together, so save the time of inserting pins.

You need to know where the scant 1/4" seam allowance is on your overlock machine. Follow the same steps of construction that are used for sewing machines starting with step #5 on page 63.

## HOW THE TEMPLATES WORK TOGETHER

It will seem like something is wrong when you place the templates A, B, C, and D next to each other. **Right, there is something wrong.** They will not fit until you sew the pieces together with a scant 1/4" seam allowance.

Also notice in the diagram to the right that template A and F are used twice in each block.

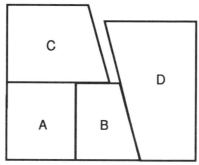

Pieces before they are sewn together with a scant 1/4"

One completed block

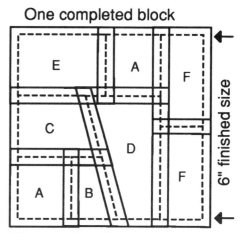

Pieces after they are sewn together with a scant 1/4"

6" finished size

## PREPARATION OF BLUE JEANS FOR RECYCLING

Step #1

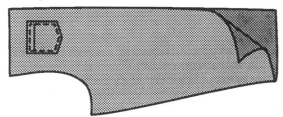

Step #1. Wash and dry the jeans. If you are going to use old blue jeans it is best if you remove the zippers and bulky seams before starting to cut out the pieces for the quilt. You might want to use parts of the pockets and the designer labels so leave them on. After you have the jeans cut apart place the leg fronts **wrong** sides together and leg backs **wrong** sides together.

I will be using the 6" (#QS7) templates in these directions. You can adapt to the 12" (#QS6) without any problems.

Step #2. You don't want to lose accuracy by disturbing the jeans and template when cutting, so allow yourself plenty of room to turn your board as you cut around the template. Make sure you have the Fabric Grips on the templates to keep them from slipping when cutting. It works best to cut on a smaller (9" x 12") Matt Board when you get down to the tiny scraps.

Step #2

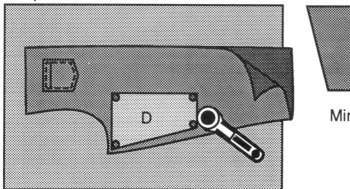

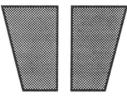

Mirror Image

If you are going to use a lot of different colors of jeans you want to cut all of the pieces needed for the quilt before you begin to sew. This way the colors are evenly distributed throughout the whole quilt instead of one area.

When you cut the pieces from the jeans with the legs wrong sides together you will get the mirror image. This will give you more options when sewing the quilt together and it will make it more interesting because you will be able to use both the right and wrong side of the jeans. You just have to remember to cut equal amounts of each of the pieces. **A and F are an exception** because they are used twice in each block, so cut twice as many of them. Cut until you have enough for the quilt size you want to make.

## 61

Step #3

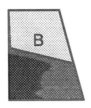

## CUTTING FROM SCRAPS OR PRE - SEWN FABRIC CRUMBS

Step #3. Layer up to six fabric scraps on top of each other and cut out the pieces.

If you want your Crazy Quilt to look even more traditional, you can pre-sew fabric crumbs together before cutting out the pieces. It will be easier to turn as you cut around the template if you use a 9" x 12" Matt Board Base.

## NUMBER OF STRIPS TO CUT USING EIGHT NEW FABRICS

You will need 64 - 6" square blocks to get a 48" x 48" quilt. This is the size before adding the border. Using 8 different fabrics makes it easy to evenly distribute the fabrics throughout the quilt. This is only a guide to follow. You can make the quilt as big as you want.

If you are using new fabric cut a strip from each of the 8 fabrics the width needed for each of the 6 templates A - F.

These fabric amounts are calculated using fabric widths of 45". Allow more or less if different widths are used.

| Template | # of strips to cut | strip width | # of pieces needed of each fabric |
|----------|--------------------|-------------|-----------------------------------|
| A | 1 | 2 1/2" | 16 |
| B | 1 | 2 1/2" | 8 |
| C | 1 | 2 1/2" | 8 |
| D | 1 | 4 1/2" | 8 |
| E | 1 | 2 1/2" | 8 |
| F | 1 | 3 1/2" | 16 |

## CUTTING THE PIECES FROM NEW FABRIC

Step #4

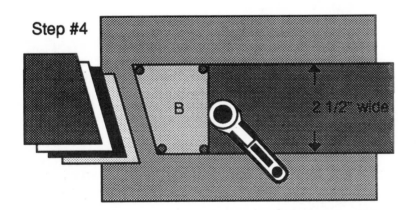

Step #4. Layer up to four of the 2 1/2" strips on top of each other and make sure the edges of the strips are lined up. Place template B on top of the strips and flip flop the template working your way across the strips.

Repeat this step with each of the templates until you have used all of the cut strips.

## SEWING INSTRUCTIONS

Before starting to sew this quilt lay out a row of 8 blocks placing the fabrics that are alike in different spots in each of the blocks. Pick up each of the blocks and keep them separated from each other.

# SEWING STEPS WHEN USING A SEWING MACHINE

### Step #5

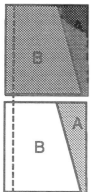
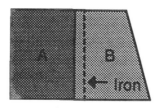

Step #5. You won't need to use pins until you sew the rows together in step #12. Finger pin an A and B right sides together and chain using a scant 1/4" seam allowance.

Press this seam in either direction.

### Step #6

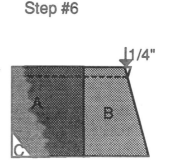
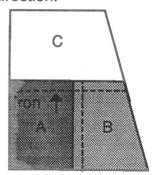

Step #6. With right sides together add a C Piece to the A and B. As shown in the diagram the C piece will have a tail extended on one end.

Iron this seam up towards the C.

### Step #7

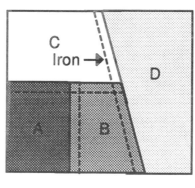

Step #7. With right sides together add piece D. There will be a tail extended on the top and bottom making allowance for the 1/4" seam allowance included in the pieces.

Iron this seam towards the D.

Step #8. Sew an E and A right sides together. Iron this seam in either direction.

Next attach the A and E to the top or bottom of the block. The A and E could also be turned 180° before sewn on. Iron this seam towards the A and E.

Step #9. With right sides together sew 2 F's together. Iron this seam in either direction.

### Step #8

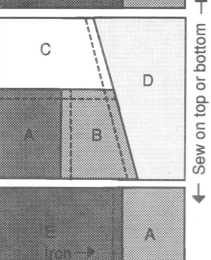

### Step #9

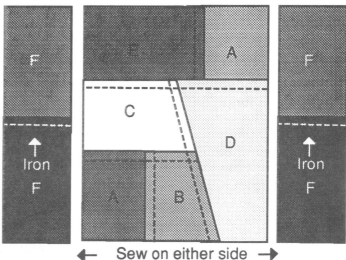

← Sew on either side →

**Step #10**

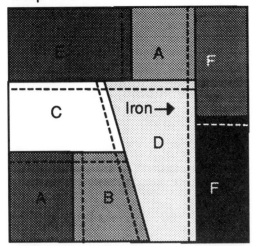

Step #10. Attach the two F's to either side of the block. Iron this seam towards the F's.

The block will now measure 6 1/2" if you are using the QS 7 template set or 12 1/2" if you are using the QS6 template set.

**Step #11**

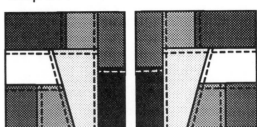

Mirror Image

Step #11. If you have cut pieces with the fabrics facing each other the blocks will be a mirror image of each other when sewn.

**Step #12**

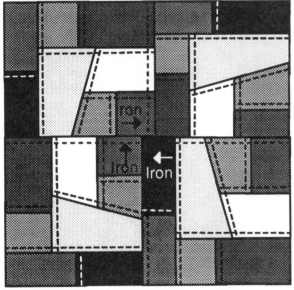

Step # 12. When sewing the blocks together, turn them a 1/4 of a turn so you lose track of the pieces. Mix in blocks that have the mirror image and blocks that have been sewn together in different ways. Sew the blocks together to form rows the length you want.

After the blocks are sewn into rows alternate the direction you iron the seams in every other row.

Step #13. Add one or more borders to the outside edge of the quilt. If you choose to use two borders the quilt will look better if you use two different border widths. Look at pages 42 and 43 to see how to add the borders.

# CRAZY QUILT

**YARDAGE REQUIREMENTS:
FINISHED SIZE 54" X 54"**
2/3 yd. of 8 different fabrics
3 yds. for borders, bindings and backing

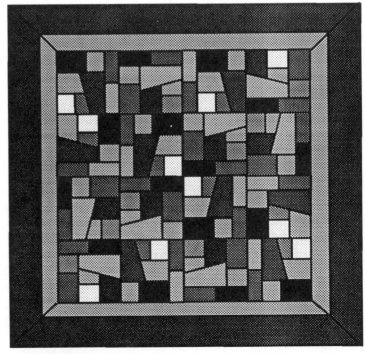

# BOW TIE

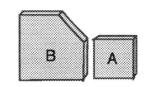

## Supplies Needed:
*6" (QS18) Bow Tie templates
*Rotary Cutter
*Matt Board Cutting Base
*6" x 24" Omnigrid Ruler
*IBC Glass Head Pins #5003

**READ PAGES 3 - 4 BEFORE STARTING THE QUILT**

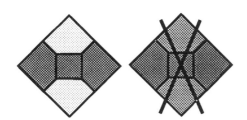

### CHOOSING THE FABRIC

The Bow Tie pattern is made up of only two pattern pieces but because there are so many different ways to arrange this block the possibilities are endless with this design. Make sure that you choose fabrics with enough contrast so the pieces in the block don't mush together. Plaids and stripes separated into light and dark groups and arranged into a mosaic tile design will look just like an antique right out of a trunk or recycle out dated ties and use them in the bow tie block.

In this project we are going to arrange the bow tie block to form Christmas wreaths. You will want to choose a bright fabric for the bow (I used a red check) which is at the top of each wreath. Then choose a Christmas print for the wreath (I used a green print) which is the darkest fabric in the bottom three blocks and a light fabric for the background.

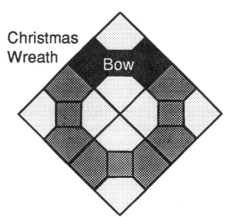

Christmas Wreath

Bow

### NUMBER OF STRIPS TO CUT
Cut 1 - 3 1/2" strip for bows (red)
Cut 1 - 2 7/8" strips for bows (red)
Cut 3 - 3 1/2" strips for wreaths (green)
Cut 2 - 2 7/8" strips for wreaths (green)
Cut 4 - 3 1/2" strips for background (beige)

### NUMBER OF PIECES NEEDED
You need 12 B's (red)
You need 6 A's (red)
You need 36 B's (green)
You need 18 A's (green)
You need 48 B's (beige)

Step #1. Place the 2 7/8" strips on top of each other and make sure that the edges of the strips are lined up. Place template A on top of the strips and cut the number of pieces needed.

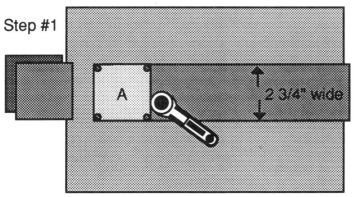

Step #1

2 3/4" wide

Step #2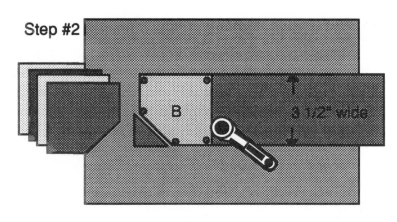

Step #2. Place four of the 3 1/2" strips on top of each other and make sure that the edges of the strips are in line. Place template B on top of the strips and cut the number of pieces needed.

**SEWING STEPS**

For this quilt you will need to make 6 blocks with the bow fabric in it for the top of each of the wreaths and 18 blocks for the wreaths.

Step #3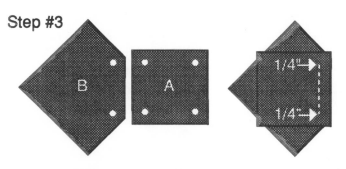

Step #3. On each of the corners of the pieces you might want to put a dot to mark the 1/4" point until you learn where to insert the pins. With right sides together place an A (square) on top of the B piece. Insert a pin 1/4" from each of the corners.
Sew this seam with a scant 1/4" and back stitch at each end.

Step #4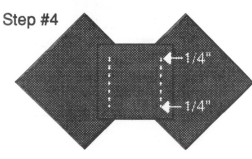

Step #4. Attach the next B piece and back stitch at each end of the seam.

Step #5. Next with right sides together add a background (beige) B piece. Sew with the square on top so you can see where to stop at the beginning and end of this seam. Do not sew past the dot you put in the corner. Back stitch at each end of this seam.

Step #6. Repeat step #5 and add the second light background B piece.

Step #5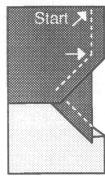

Step #6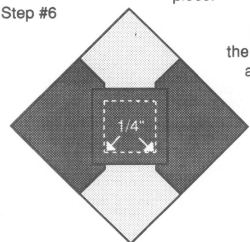

Step #7. Fold the block in half and starting from the outside edge sew the seam that connects the B's together. Back stitch in the center of the block at the point the seams meet. Repeat this step until you have all four of these seams sewn.

Step #7

Step #8. Iron the seams in one direction as indicated by the arrows.

Step #8

Step #9

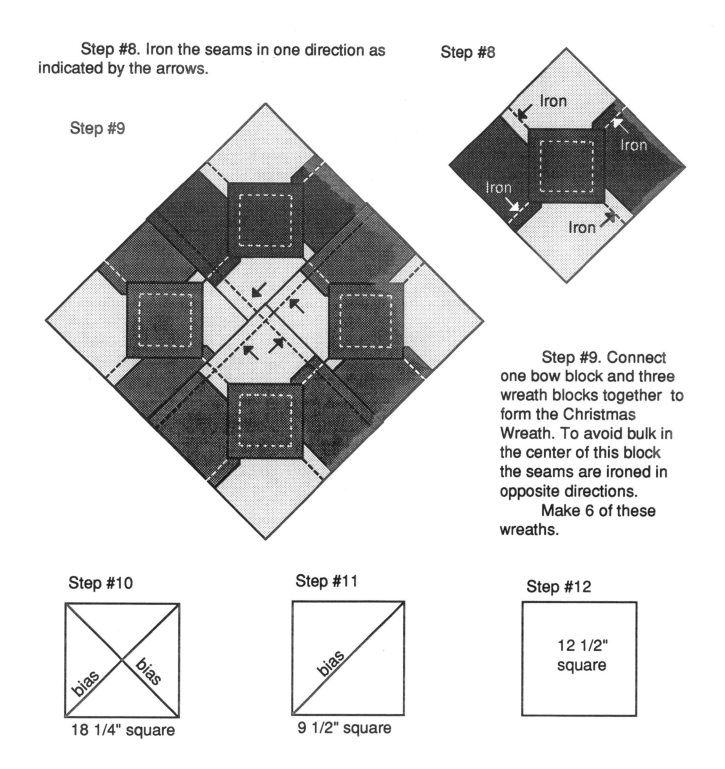

Iron

Iron

Iron

Iron

Step #9. Connect one bow block and three wreath blocks together to form the Christmas Wreath. To avoid bulk in the center of this block the seams are ironed in opposite directions.

Make 6 of these wreaths.

Step #10

bias    bias

18 1/4" square

Step #11

bias

9 1/2" square

Step #12

12 1/2" square

Step #10. To keep the quilt from stretching out of shape when finished, cut the side triangles and corner triangles so that the bias edges will be on the inside seams and the straight of grain on the outside edge of the quilt.

From the background fabric cut 2 - 18 1/4" squares. Cut them again on the diagonal in both directions. You will get four side triangles from each square.

Step #11. From the background fabric cut 2 - 9 1/2" squares and cut them again in half on the diagonal for the corner triangles.

Step #12. From the background fabric cut 2 - 12 1/2" squares for the center part of the quilt.

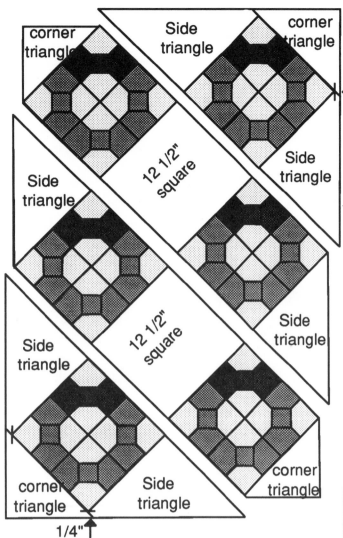

corner triangle

Side triangle

corner triangle

← 1/4"

12 1/2" square

Side triangle

Side triangle

Side triangle

12 1/2" square

Side triangle

Side triangle

Side triangle

corner triangle

Side triangle

corner triangle

1/4"

Step #13. Sew the blocks and triangles into rows as shown in the diagram.

Iron the seams in every other row in opposite directions to avoid bulk in the corners when sewing the rows together.

Step #14. Sew the rows together.

Do not trim off the 1/4" seam allowance on the edges after you have sewn on the triangles because you need it when you add the border.

If you use two borders cut the strips for the inside one (red) 1" wide and the outside border (green) 4" wide.

Look at page 42 & 43 to see how to attach the border.

# *BOW TIE*

**SHOWN IN COLOR ON PAGE 52**
**FINISHED SIZE: 40 1/2" X 57 1/2"**
**FABRIC REQUIREMENTS:**
*1/4 yd. for bows (red)
*1 3/4 yd. for background (beige)
*1/2 yd. for wreaths (green)
*2 1/2 yds. for the quilt back and outside borders (green)
*1/2 yd. inside border (optional) and binding (red)

# KALEIDOSCOPE

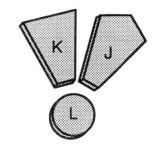

## Supplies Needed:
* QS4 (large) or QS5 (small) Dresden Plate template set
* Rotary Cutter
* Large Matt Board Cutting Base & 6" x 8" or 9" x 12" Matt Board
* 6" x 24" or 6" x 12" Omnigrid Ruler

### READ PAGES 3 - 4 BEFORE STARTING THIS QUILT

### CHOOSING FABRIC FOR THE CHRISTMAS TREE SKIRT OR TABLE CLOTH

I have named this quilt after the Kaleidoscope instrument which one turns to create many different symmetrical designs. You will discover that by changing the placement of color or by rotating the blocks you can create many illusions.

Choose fabrics that have a variety of background and print so that the pieces don't mush together. You will get the best Kaleidoscope design if you use light, medium and dark fabrics.

### NUMBER OF STRIPS TO CUT FOR (LARGE) FINISHED SIZE 52 1/2" CIRCLE

Cut 4 strips  5 1/2" wide x 45" long for template J
Cut 1 strip 4 1/2" wide x 45" long for template K

Cut 3 strips 5 1/2" wide x 45" long for template J
Cut 2 strips 4" wide x 45" long for template L

Cut 1 strip 5 1/2" wide x 45" long for template J
Cut 6 strips 4 1/2' wide x 45" long for template K

### NUMBER OF STRIPS TO CUT FOR THE (SMALL) FINISHED SIZE 25 3/4" CIRCLE

Cut 2 strips 3" wide x 45" for template J
Cut 1 strip 2 1/2" wide x  45" long for template K

Cut 2 strips 3" wide x 45" long for template J
Cut 1 strip 2" wide x 45" long for template L

Cut 1 strip 3" wide x 45" long for template J
Cut 4 strips 2 1/2" wide x 45" long for template K

### NUMBER OF PIECES NEEDED FROM EACH FABRIC FOR (LARGE OR SMALL)

| J | K | L |
|---|---|---|
| 60 | 12 | 19 |
| 48 | 0 | |
| 6 | 102 | |

Step #1

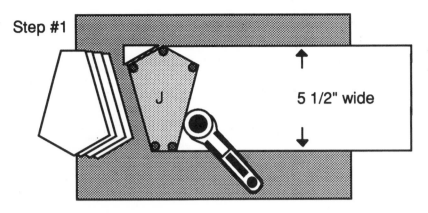

5 1/2" wide

Step #1. Layer the 5 1/2" (large) or 3" (small) strips on top of each other and make sure that the edges are in line. Place template J on top of the strips and use the Rotary Cutter to make the long cut first. Then cut off the ears. To save fabric, flip flop the template working your way across the strips until they are all cut up. Look at the chart on page 69 to see how many of each color to cut.

Step #2

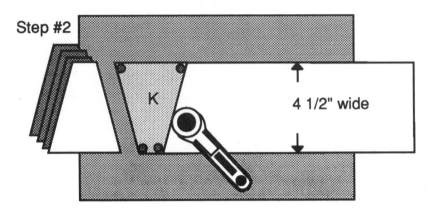

4 1/2" wide

Step #2. Layer the 4 1/2" (large) or 2 1/2" (small) strips on top of each other and make sure that the edges are in line. Place template K on top of these strips and cut along the edge of the template with the Rotary Cutter. Flip flop the template until all the strips are used.

Step #3

Step #3. Before cutting the circles cut the fabric into 4" squares (for large) or 2" squares (for small) so you don't have to handle so much fabric when you cut out the circles. If you use a 6" x 8" or 9" x 12" matt board base to cut on you will be able to turn the board as you cut your way around the circles. Place template L on top of 4 - 6 squares and with short cuts and turns cut out the circles. The small cutter will work best.

## SEWING STEPS

Step #4. Completely read steps 4 - 9 before starting. The diagram shows how to arrange the pieces to form each of the blocks and tells how many of each you need to make. Work on one block combination at a time.

Step #4

Sew 1 of these for the center

Sew 6 of these for the second row

Sew 6 of these for the third row

Sew 6 of these for the third row

**Step #5**

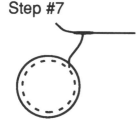

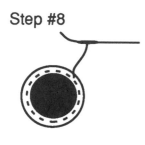

Step #5. With right sides together place a K on top of a J. Match up the narrow edge and there will be a tail at the top of the K. Starting at the wide end, chain sew K's and J's together with a **scant 1/4"** until you have 6 sets which is enough for the center block. Do not back stitch and always sew with the same piece (K) on top to keep the pieces in the correct order in the block.

Step #6. Next, chain sew them into 3 groups of four. Sew the groups of 4 together until all 12 pieces are connected. Make sure every other piece in the block is a J and K.

Iron all the seams in the same direction.

**Step #6**

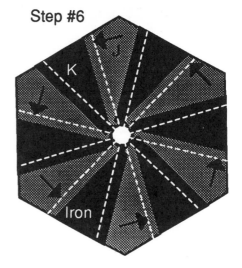

**Step #7**

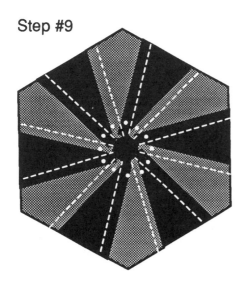

Step #7. With a needle and thread make a running stitch (**with short stitches 1/8" apart**) 1/8" from the outside edge around the complete circle. If the stitches are too long the circle won't have smooth edges when ironed. Leave a 3" piece of thread to grab on to in the next step.

Step #8. With a compass draw a circle on a light weight cardboard a 1/4" smaller than template L and cut it out.

Next, place the cardboard in the center of the circle and draw up the thread from the running stitch until the fabric is snug around the cardboard. The center circle should now be 1/4" smaller than template L. Press the circle on both the right and wrong sides to hold the shape. Do not remove the cardboard.

Step #9. With the cardboard still inside, center the circle from step #8 under a block with the wrong sides up and insert a pin on every piece to secure the cardboard to the block.

**Step #8**

**Step #9**

### OOPS! ANOTHER SEWING TEST!

If the circle does not cover the hole in the center of the block the seams are too narrow. If the circle seams too big for the block you have made the seams too deep

When the circle fits the block you are ready to connect them together. Use a matching thread and attach the circle by hand using a whip with stitches 1/8" apart. Remove the cardboard after the circle is attached.

If you are going to attach the circle with the sewing machine remove the cardboard first. Set the machine on a blind hemming stitch and use an invisible nylon filament thread.

Continue Steps 5 and 9 until you have made all of the blocks needed in Step #4.

## 71

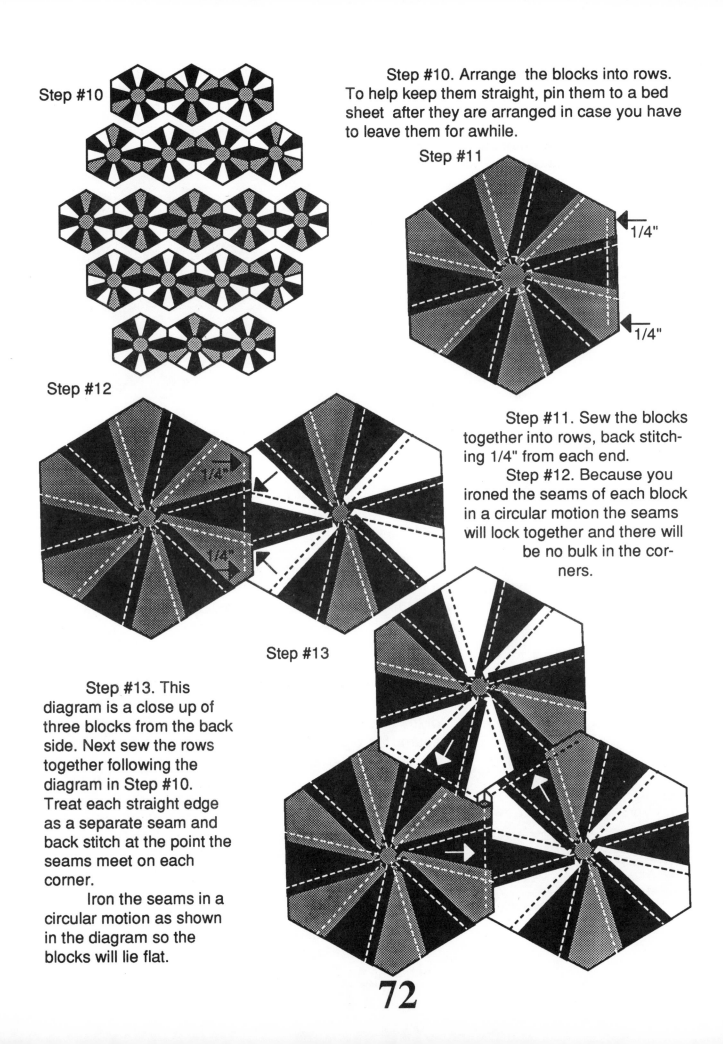

Step #10

Step #10. Arrange the blocks into rows. To help keep them straight, pin them to a bed sheet after they are arranged in case you have to leave them for awhile.

Step #11

1/4"

1/4"

Step #11. Sew the blocks together into rows, back stitching 1/4" from each end.

Step #12. Because you ironed the seams of each block in a circular motion the seams will lock together and there will be no bulk in the corners.

Step #12

1/4"

1/4"

Step #13

Step #13. This diagram is a close up of three blocks from the back side. Next sew the rows together following the diagram in Step #10. Treat each straight edge as a separate seam and back stitch at the point the seams meet on each corner.

Iron the seams in a circular motion as shown in the diagram so the blocks will lie flat.

72

Step #13. After you have the hand or machine quilting done, you can make it into a Christmas tree skirt by cutting from the outside edge to the center. If you have an artificial tree you could leave out the center circle. If you make the cut before it is quilted it will be very difficult to handle.

Look at page 79 to see how to put the binding on.

Step #13

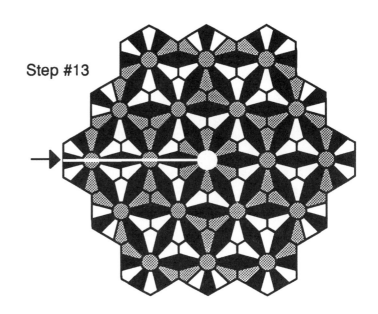

# KALEIDOSCOPE

## CHRISTMAS TREE SKIRT OR TABLE CLOTH

**SHOWN IN COLOR ON PAGE 52**
**FINISHED SIZE 52 1/2" CIRCLE**
**FABRIC REQUIREMENTS:**

☐ 1 yd. light
▨ 3/4 yd. medium
■ 1 yd. dark
■ 6 yds. for back and binding

**FINISHED SIZE 25 3/4"**
**FABRIC REQUIREMENTS:**

1/3 yd. light
☐ 1/3 yd. medium
▨ 1/2 yd. dark
■ 1 yd. dark for back and binding
■

# DRUNKARD'S PATH

## Supplies Needed:
* 4" (QS13) or 3" (QS12) templates
* Small Rotary Cutter (works best)
* 6" x 24" or 6" x 12" Omnigrid Ruler
* Large Matt Board Cutting Base
* Small Matt Board Cutting Base (9" x 12")
* IBC Glass Head Pins #5003

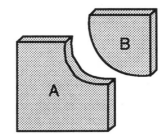

**READ PAGES 3 - 4 BEFORE STARTING THE QUILT**

## CHOOSING FABRICS FOR THE LOVE RING VARIATION OF THE DRUNKARD'S PATH

Step #1

Step #1. There are just two pattern pieces in each block. The pie shaped piece in some of the blocks will be dark and in some it will be light.

Step #2. Next, these single blocks will be arranged to form a Love Ring block. You can make it in either the 3" or 4" size. The 4" is best for the bed quilts and the 3" is a nicer size for wall quilts. It takes 36 single blocks to make up one complete Love Ring.

Step #2

24" finished block when using the 4" templates
18" finished block when using the 3" templates

You can make this quilt to look like an antique that has come right out of a trunk in grandma's attic by using scraps from other quilting and sewing projects. You can mix in stripes, plaids, paisleys, dots, or any design found in fabric. I do suggest however that you use all 100% cotton fabrics.

Step #3. Make sure that you use only the medium and dark fabrics for the darkest part of the design.

A tea died fabric would look nice for the light part of the block if you want it to look old.

To avoid the pieces from mushing together which would ruin this design. Leave the light scraps for another quilt.

Step #3

If you like contemporary quilts you might want to choose a large floral print for the dark part of the block and a light complementary print for the light part of the Love Ring design. I personally like both the antique and contemporary look. Where and how you are going to use this quilt will determine the fabric choices you make.

## 74

## Step #4

There are 16 of these in each block

There are 20 of these in each block

Step #4. You will need the same amount of each of these blocks regardless if you use scraps or new fabric to make one Love Ring block. After you have decided which size template you are going to use and how big you want to make the quilt, multiply the number of Love Ring blocks needed times the number of pieces needed for each Love Ring block.

## CUTTING THE PIECES FROM SCRAPS

## Step #5

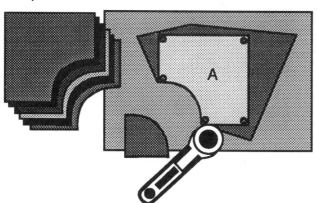

Step #5. Using a 9" x 12" Matt Board base to cut on will give you the ability to turn the board easily as you cut out the pieces. Place the template on top of as many as 6 fabric scraps and, with a small (works best on curves) Rotary Cutter, cut around the template.

## CUTTING FROM NEW FABRICS

## Step #6

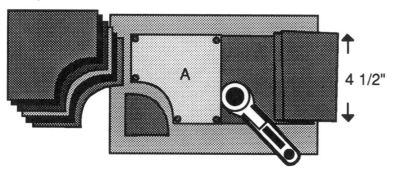

4 1/2"

Step #6. Cut strips (4 1/2" wide for the 4" finished block or 3 1/2" wide for the 3" finished block). Layer the strips (as many as six) on top of each other and make sure the edges line up. Bifold these strips on a smaller 9" x 12" Matt Board so you can turn your work as you cut around the template. Flip flop template A across the strips until they are all used up.

## Step #7

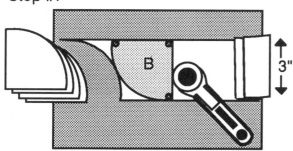

3"

Step #7. Cut strips (3"wide for the 4" finished block or 2 1/2" wide for the 3" finished block) and layer up to six on top of each other. Make sure the edges of the strips are lined up. Bifold the strips on a small 9" x 12" Matt Board because it is a benefit to be able to turn your work as you cut around the template. When you flip flop template B (look at the diagram) turn it so that you can get the most use of the fabric.

## SEWING STEPS

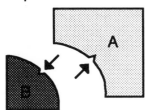

Step #8

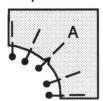

Step #10

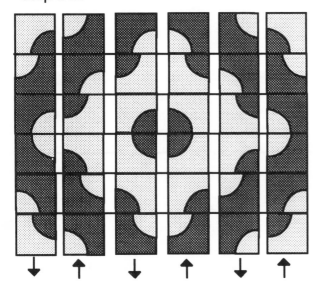

Step #8. Fold the A and B piece in half and cut a notch to mark the center. Be careful not to cut it too deep.

Step #9. With right sides together match up the notches of the A and B piece.

Step #10. It works best for me to work with the A piece on top. First put a pin in the middle, then a pin at each end and one or two inbetween. When I put the point of the pin in right on the 1/4" seam allowance this seam is easier to sew.

Step #11. Sew this seam with a scant 1/4" seam allowance. To set the seam, first finger press, then iron it toward the B piece.

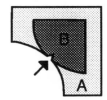

Step #9

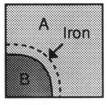

Step #11

Step #12

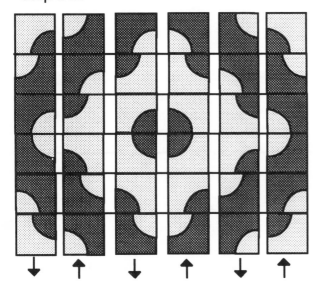

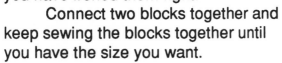

Step #12. Arrange the pieces the way that you want them in the block and pin them together. After you have pinned them into rows, chain sew them together. **Do not clip the threads** between each of the rows.

Iron the seams in opposite directions as indicated by the arrows in every other row.

Step#13. Finger pin as you sew the rows together to form the Love Ring block. The seams will lock together if you have ironed them right.

Connect two blocks together and keep sewing the blocks together until you have the size you want.

Look on page 42-43 to see how to put on the borders.

Step #13

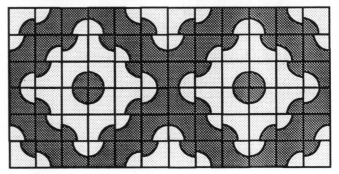

76

# LOVE RING WALL QUILT

**FINISHED SIZE:**
**USING THE 3" TEMPLATES**
**36" X 36" (WITHOUT BORDERS)**

**FABRIC REQUIREMENTS**
1 1/4 yds. of the light
use scraps for the dark part of the design
1 1/2 yds. for the border and back

*If you want to use only two colors
1 1/4 yd. of the light
1 1/4 yd. of the dark
1 1/2 yd. for the border and back

**USING THE 4" TEMPLATES IT IS**
**48" X 48" (WITHOUT BORDERS)**

**FABRIC REQUIREMENTS:**
1 3/4 Yds. of the light
Use scraps for the dark part of the design
2 Yds. for the border and back

*If you want to use only two colors
1 3/4 yd. of the light
2 yds. of the dark
2 yds. for the border and back

**THIS DIAGRAM SHOWS WHAT**
**WILL HAPPEN WHEN YOU**
**REVERSE THE COLORS IN THE**
**LOVE RING QUILT**

# FINISHING THE QUILT

When your quilt top is finished you need to give some thought on how you want to finish it. You can make the quilt sandwich by securing the quilt top, batting and back by machine or hand-quilting or by tying it with square knots in the corners of the blocks.

## CHOOSE THE QUILTING DESIGNS BEFORE MAKING THE QUILT SANDWICH

If you are going to hand or machine quilt you need to choose quilting designs. The quilting will show up more on the solid fabrics than on prints. There are many plastic template quilting designs available and many of them are made just for borders. Pick the designs that relate to the design in the quilt top you have made. Also try to pick designs that will fill the space nicely.

In some areas you might want to just stitch 1/4" away from the seam to accentuate the shapes and in other areas fill in with some cross hatching (lines that are crossed diagonally to fill an area). I use a yard stick to follow when putting these lines on the quilt.

After you have decided what you are going to do you need to mark the designs on the quilt top. I like to place a fine sandpaper under the quilt top to keep it from moving around while I'm marking it. Test the marking pencil you plan to use on a scrap of fabric to make sure that it can be removed before using it. I do not recommend that you use water-soluble pens or the disappearing marking pens because it can get into the batting making it difficult to remove. I mark lightly with a #2 lead pencil or chalk pencils. Mark the entire top before making the quilt sandwich (putting the three layers together).

## PREPARE THE BACK OF A QUILT

If you have used light fabrics in the top of the quilt do not use a dark fabric for the quilt back because it will show through. Before making the quilt sandwich (front, batting, & backing) you will need to make the back for the quilt. This should be 2"-3" larger on all four sides than the front. Measure the quilt top and add 4" to 6" to the length and the width. If you are making a wall quilt that is less than 40" wide you will not have to sew strips of fabric together for the backing, You would just cut the length you need. If your quilt is wider than 40" you have to sew strips of fabric together.

Measure the quilt for which you are making the back and figure out the best use of fabric. The length and width of the quilt will determine whether you put the center seam (or seams) lengthwise or crosswise on the back of the quilt.

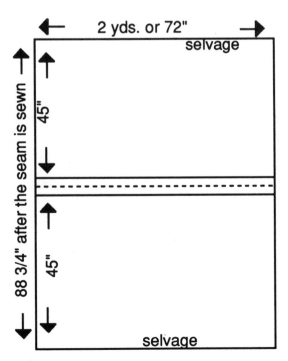

Diagram labels: 2 yds. or 72" — selvage — 45" — 45" — 88 3/4" after the seam is sewn — selvage

## EXAMPLE OF A QUILT BACK FOR CLOVER ALL OVER FINISHED SIZE 66" WIDE X 75" LONG

It is best to put the seam going across the center width of this quilt because there will be less waste of fabric that way. Cut 2 lengths of fabric 45" wide x 2 yds. long. This length will allow 3" extra on each side of the quilt. You will have about

6 3/4" extra on the top and bottom. Trim it so there is only 3" extra on the top and bottom. Keep the seam in the middle.

Sew this seam with right sides together and a  5/8" seam allowance. Trim off the selvage edge to 1/4" after the seam is sewn.  Never use the selvage edge in a quilt because it is too tightly woven and it will create pucker problems. Press the seam open.

## QUILT SANDWICH

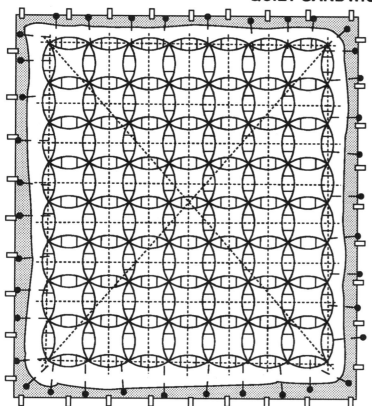

Put the back of the quilt on the bottom with the **wrong side facing up.** The middle is the batting and the pieced quilt is on the top, **right side facing up.**

Work on a table top or a tile floor if available. Smooth out and secure the bottom layer in place (wrong side up) with masking tape. The batting and pieced top is secured in place with pins. Baste the quilt with a large needle diagonally, vertically and horizontally.

## QUILTING

After the quilt is basted it is ready to be hand-quilted. I like to put the quilt in a Q Snap frame when I'm hand quilting because it is light weight, easy to move from one spot to another and you can get into the corners so nicely.

If you don't want to baste  the quilt before hand-quilting it you need to secure it in a floor frame.

I like to use a 10 Between quilting needle when hand quilting. You might want to experiment with different size needles. The larger the number the smaller the needle.

Insert the needle 1/2" away from where you want to start stitching and give the thread a slight jerk so that the knot will end up in the batting layer. With a thimble on the middle finger and a rocking motion of the needle in your hand, put about 4-6 stitches on the needle each time before you pull up the thread. When you get to about 5" of the end of your thread you can back stitch in the same track or end with a knot pulled into the batting.

## BINDING YOUR QUILT

Look at pages 4 and 5 to see how to cut strips. If you are binding a round a quilt with curves cut the strips on the bias. After the quilt is hand or machine quilted and before you begin to attach the binding to the quilt you should either sew around  the quilt 1/4" from the outside edge with a walking foot or hand baste. This will keep the quilt and binding from puckering when you sew.

Step #1. Cut enough 2" strips of fabric to go around the quilt you are making.
Cut off both ends of all of the 2" strips at a 45° angle so that when they are sewn together the bulk of the seam will be evenly distributed. Sew the strips together and press the seams open.

At the beginning of the binding fold 1/4" back and press.

Step #1

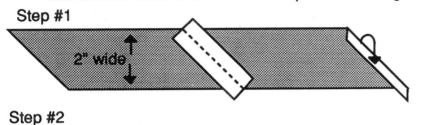

Step #2. Fold the binding in half and press.

Step #2

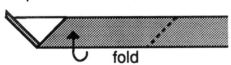

fold

Step #3. Starting with the end of the binding that has the 1/4" folded back, place the binding on the **right side** of the quilt. Make sure that a seam does not fall on a corner, if it does find a new place to start. Match up the edge of the quilt to the cut edge of the binding and start sewing 1" after the 1/4" fold so that the end of the binding can be slipped inside when you get to it for a nice finish. **Do not stretch the binding as you sew it on the quilt.** Sew 1/4" from the edge and stop sewing 1/4" from the corner of the quilt edge and back stitch.

Step #3

↓Start here    ↓Stop 1/4" from corner

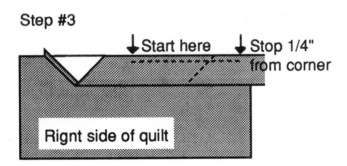

Rignt side of quilt

Step #4. Turn your work and fold the binding back. The binding edge and quilt edge should make a straight line when it is folded regardless of the angle of the quilt corner. This fold will start the miter on the corner.

Step #4

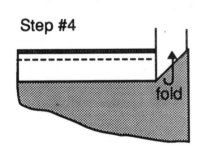

fold

Step #5. Place your finger on the first fold and flip the binding down to make the second fold even with the binding, this will complete the miter. Finger pin and start sewing from the outside edge and sew to 1/4" of the next corner. Repeat Steps #3 - #5 until you are around the complete quilt.

Step #5

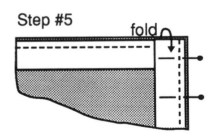

fold

Step #6. Next turn the binding on the right side to the back side of the quilt to form the miter.

Step #6

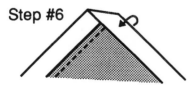

Step #7. Fold the other side over to complete the mitered corner. The bulk in the corners will automatically end opposite each other on the top and bottom. Using a matching thread sew with a blind stitch to finish off your heirloom.

Step #7

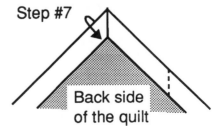

Back side of the quilt

If you are attaching binding to curves, stop with the needle down on the inner most point between two curves. Readjust the quilt and binding and continue on. An inside miter will automatically be formed.

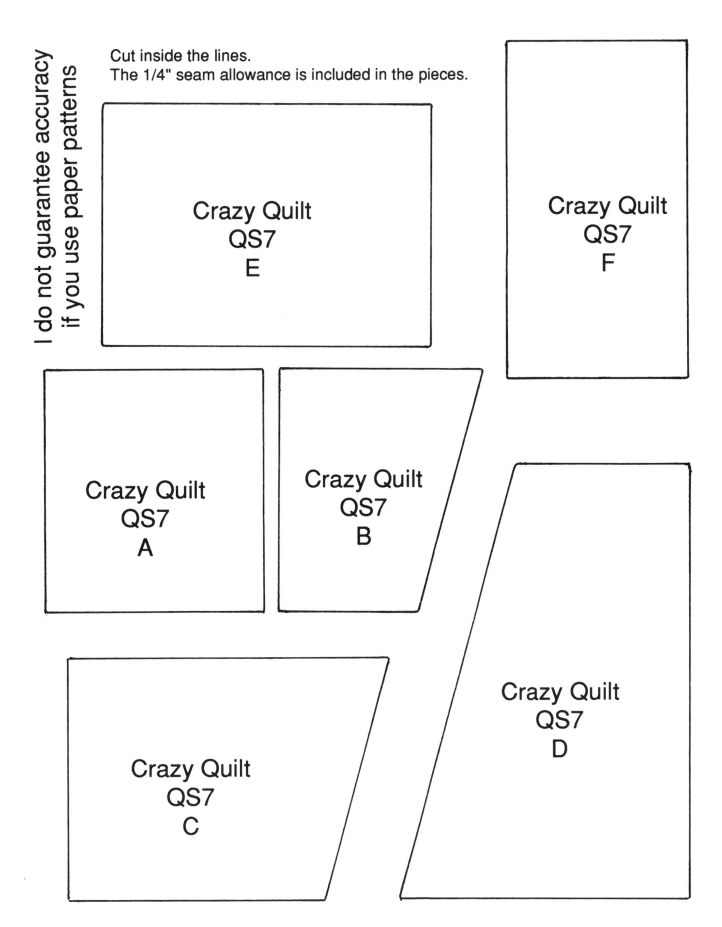

Cut inside the lines.
The 1/4" seam allowance is included in the pieces.

I do not guarantee accuracy
if you use paper patterns

Crazy Quilt
QS7
E

Crazy Quilt
QS7
F

Crazy Quilt
QS7
A

Crazy Quilt
QS7
B

Crazy Quilt
QS7
D

Crazy Quilt
QS7
C

Cut inside the lines.
The 1/4" seam allowance is included in the pieces.

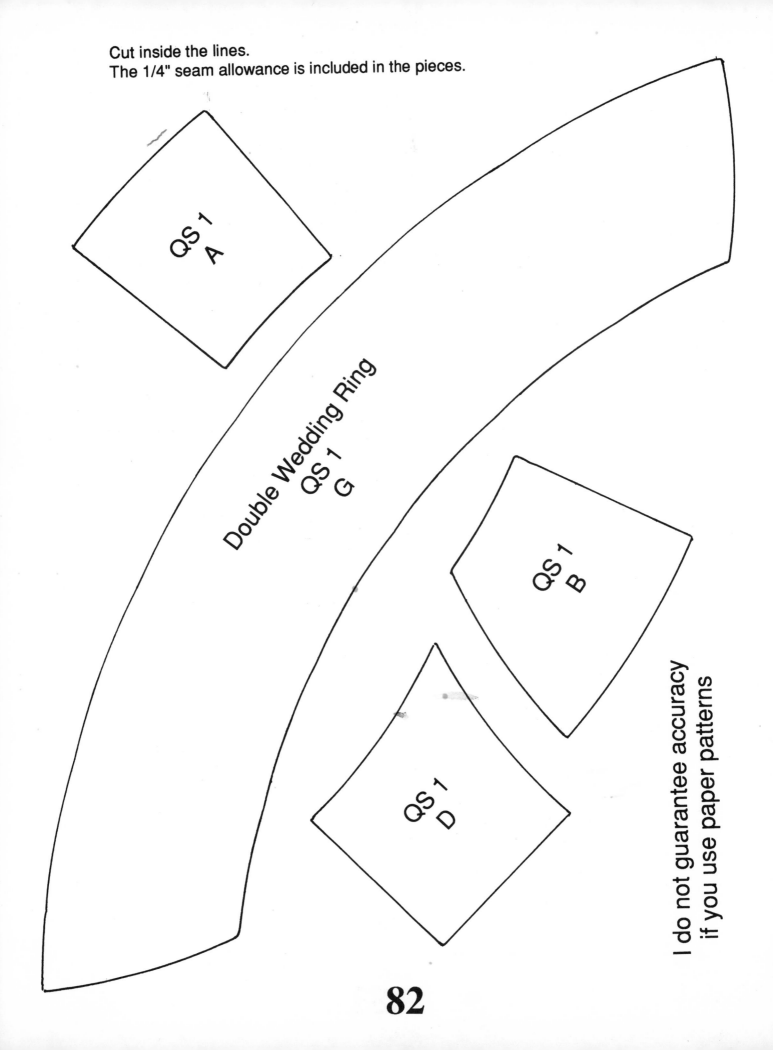

QS 1
A

Double Wedding Ring
QS 1
G

QS 1
B

QS 1
D

I do not guarantee accuracy
if you use paper patterns

82

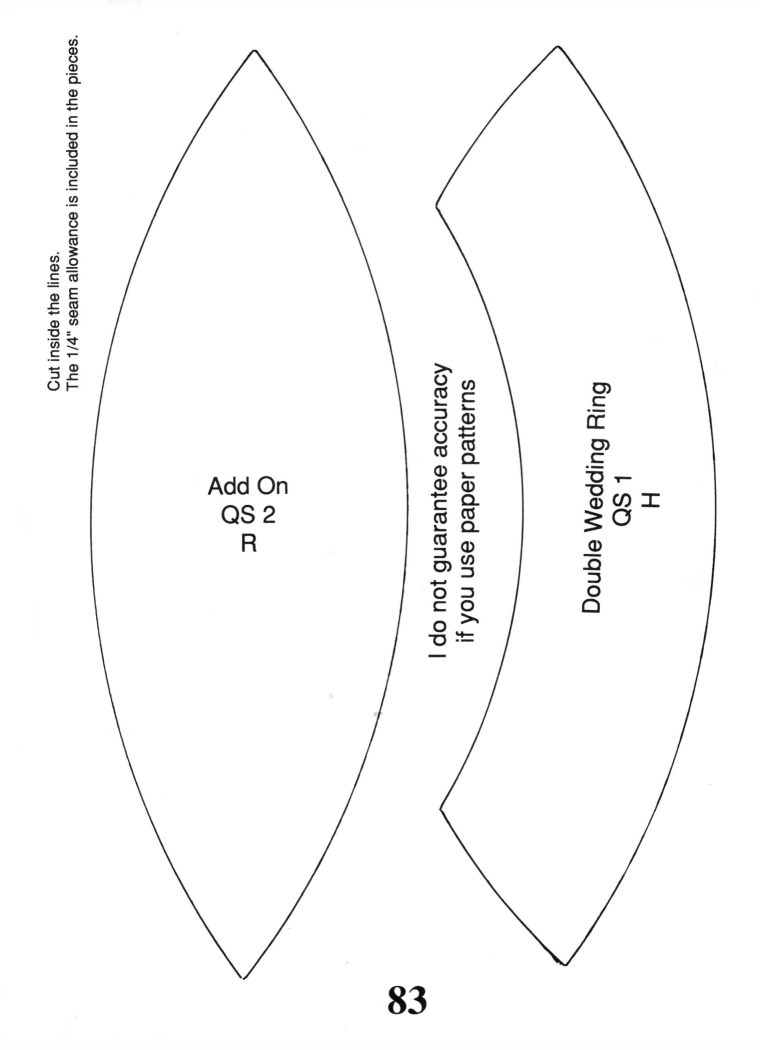

Cut inside the lines.
The 1/4" seam allowance is included in the pieces.

Add On
QS 2
R

I do not guarantee accuracy
if you use paper patterns

Double Wedding Ring
QS 1
H

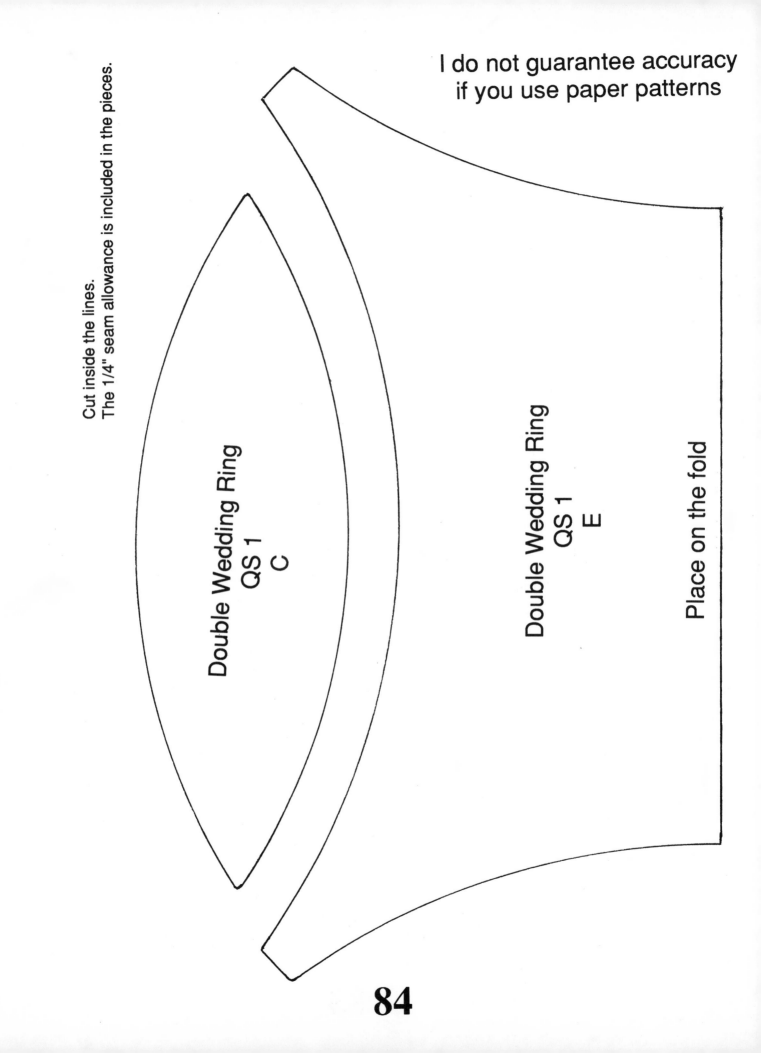

Cut inside the lines.
The 1/4" seam allowance is included in the pieces.

I do not guarantee accuracy
if you use paper patterns

Double Wedding Ring
QS 1
C

Double Wedding Ring
QS 1
E

Place on the fold

84

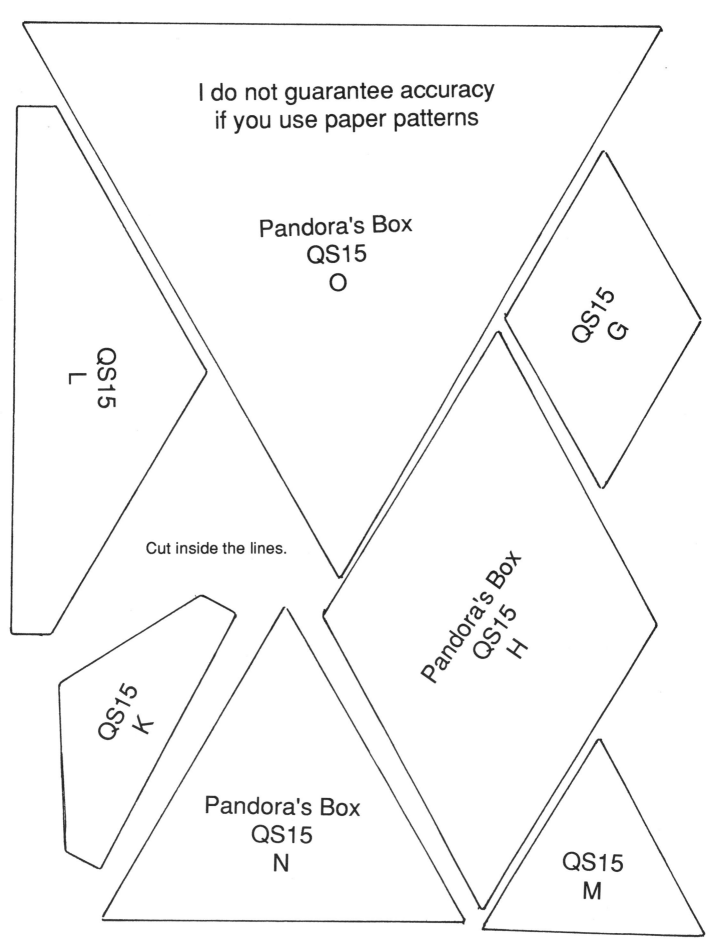

I do not guarantee accuracy
if you use paper patterns

Pandora's Box
QS15
O

QS15
G

QS15
L

Cut inside the lines.

Pandora's Box
QS15
H

QS15
K

Pandora's Box
QS15
N

QS15
M

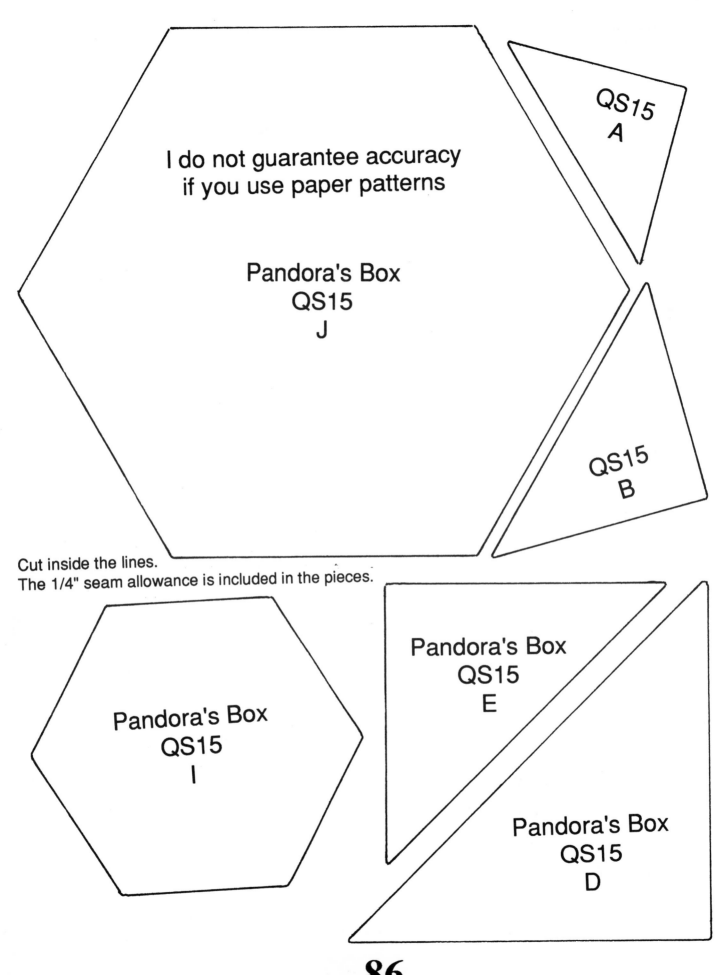

I do not guarantee accuracy
if you use paper patterns

QS15
A

Pandora's Box
QS15
J

QS15
B

Cut inside the lines.
The 1/4" seam allowance is included in the pieces.

Pandora's Box
QS15
E

Pandora's Box
QS15
I

Pandora's Box
QS15
D

**86**

Cut inside the lines.
The 1/4" seam allowance is included in the pieces.

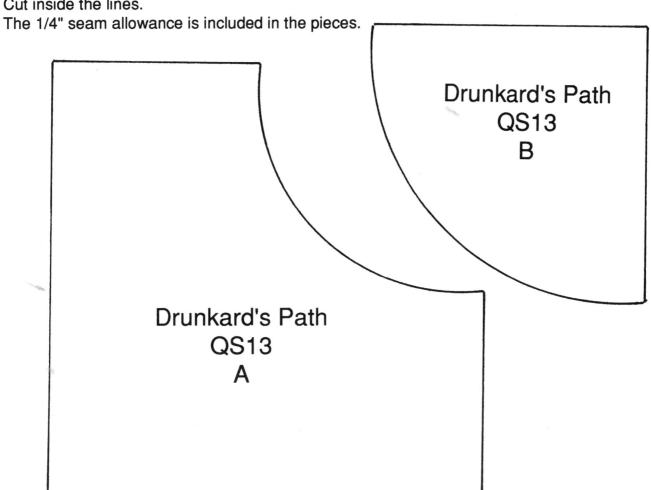

Drunkard's Path
QS13
B

Drunkard's Path
QS13
A

I do not guarantee accuracy
if you use paper patterns

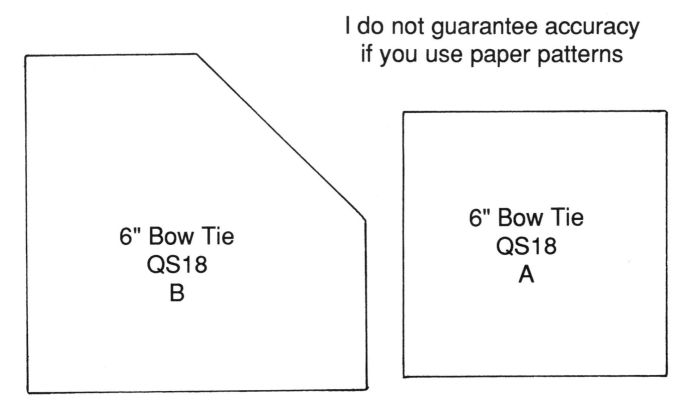

6" Bow Tie
QS18
B

6" Bow Tie
QS18
A

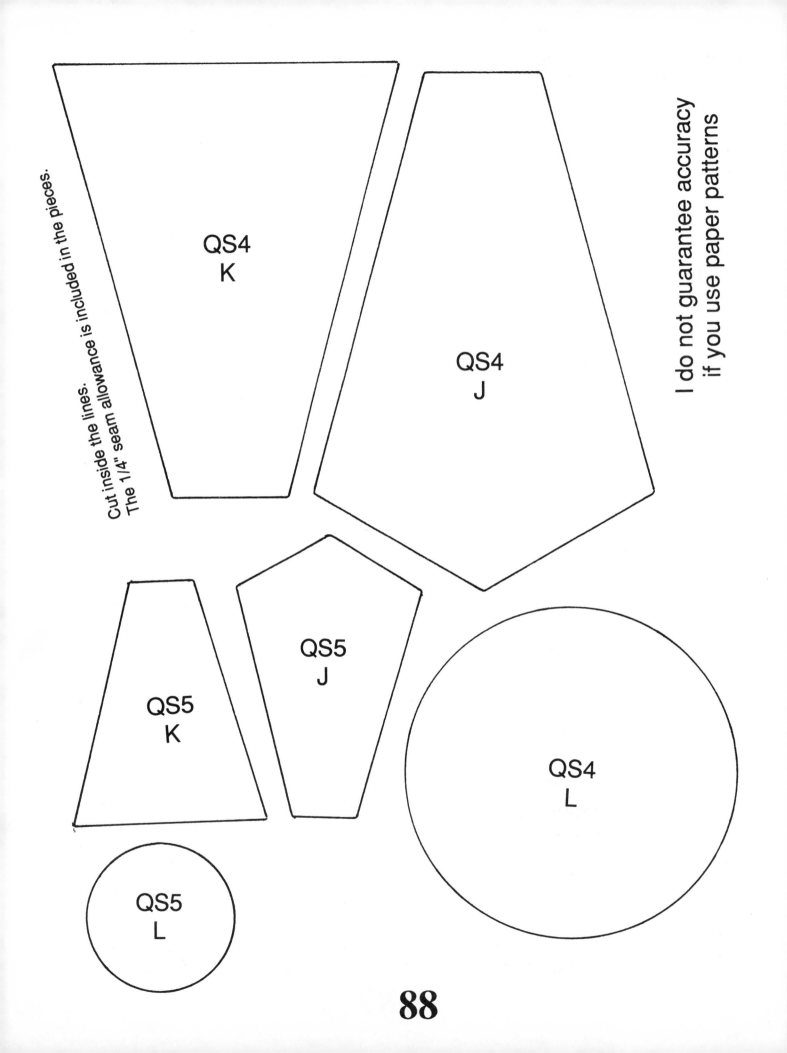

QS4
K

QS4
J

Cut inside the lines.
The 1/4" seam allowance is included in the pieces.

I do not guarantee accuracy
if you use paper patterns

QS5
J

QS5
K

QS4
L

QS5
L

# PRINTING
## For The Craft Industry

- **Pattern Covers**
- **Sell Sheets**
- **Instruction Booklets**
- **Patterns**
- **Cross Stitch Leaflets**
- **Catalogs**
- **Mini-Catalogs**

- **Discover** our special full color pattern cover and sell sheet program designed to save you time and money.

- **Special Attention** – Trained representatives to meet your printing needs. Let us know how we can better serve you.

- **National WATS Line** – 1-800-336-3504 allows you the convenience of direct contact with trained personnel.

- **Shorter Lead Time** – Less time between copy deadline and shipping date providing you with more time for packaging and marketing.

For a Free Information Brochure and Assistance, Please Call:

# 1-800-336-3504

**Palmer** Printing Company
Craft Products Division

P.O. Box 1575 • St. Cloud, MN 56302 • 612-252-0033 • Fax 612-252-9547

# QUILTERS

**Find out why these magazines are favorites of quilters everywhere!**

**Take a FREE look!**

**N**o matter what your skill level, quilting can be a rewarding experience with the help of *Quilt World, Stitch 'N Sew Quilts* and *Quick & Easy Quilting*. Venture into a new hobby or expand your talent and ideas with a subscription to one of these popular magazines!

*Quick & Easy Quilting* is the solution for the quilt lover with a busy schedule. Timesaving quilting tips and techniques enable you to create a top-quality quilt in just a short time. You'll find dozens of full-size, easy-to-follow patterns for pretty and practical quilted projects for your home, your wardrobe and your gift list.

*Stitch 'N Sew Quilts* brings you beautiful quilt patterns and blocks to make and cherish. Each issue is devoted to a specific quilting theme, enabling you to easily build a complete library of quilt patterns in no time at all. Incorporated into this magazine are the finest of the traditional patterns so loved, plus the best of fresh, new designs. Easy-to-follow patterns make quilting a pleasure!

*Quilt World* covers the best of traditional and contemporary quilting. You'll love the tried-and-true techniques and full-size patterns that help you create beautiful projects. Containing a comprehensive quilt show directory and fascinating feature stories on outstanding quilts and quilters, *Quilt World* is a favorite everywhere. Engaging full-color photos will inspire you to create quilts sure to be treasured for a lifetime! Order a subscription today!

# Omnigrid®
## Creating a Revolution in Rotary Cutting

## Rulers and Cutting Mats

## For the Quilter/Crafter

**YOU WILL LOVE OMNIGRID® RULERS' EXCLUSIVE ADVANTAGES:**

*Visibility on both dark and light materials.

*Equally usable by left- and right-handed quilters, artists, etc.

*Double 30, 45, and 60 degree angle lines that eliminate flipping and turning your ruler thus allowing maximum versatility and speed.

*Superior accuracy and design are guaranteed to give you satisfaction and quality results.

*7 sizes available for your various applications.

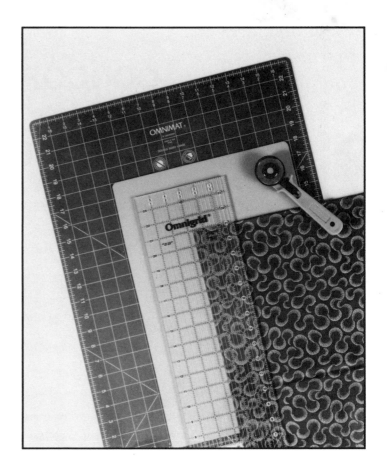

*I like to use the Omnigrid® ruler because I can measure and cut with confidence.*

*Shar*

# FABRICS USED

## IN THE QUILTING FROM THE HEARTLAND T.V. SERIES

### WERE FURNISHED IN PART BY

# BENERTEX, INC.

# VIP

# CONCORD HOUSE®

# SOUTH SEA IMPORTS